About the Author

Jula Aniol is a highly motivated and enthusiastic person with a deep passion for psychotherapy for over eleven years now. She is an integrative psychologist and psychotherapist with two MSc degrees – one in Psychology and another one in Addiction Psychology & Counselling. Her first professional years were dedicated to specializing and working in the addiction and co-dependency fields. With time and clinical experience, she gradually moved toward working with all types of trauma and she is continuing to grow her expertise in this field. Currently, she is working in Private Psychotherapy Practice based in Ramsgate.

From Co-Dependent to Independent: A Psychotherapist's Diary

Jula Aniol

From Co-Dependent to Independent: A Psychotherapist's Diary

Olympia Publishers
London

www.olympiapublishers.com
OLYMPIA PAPERBACK EDITION

Copyright © Jula Aniol 2024

The right of Jula Aniol to be identified as author of
this work has been asserted in accordance with sections 77 and 78 of
the Copyright, Designs and Patents Act 1988.

All Rights Reserved

No reproduction, copy or transmission of this publication
may be made without written permission.
No paragraph of this publication may be reproduced,
copied or transmitted save with the written permission of the publisher,
or in accordance with the provisions
of the Copyright Act 1956 (as amended).

Any person who commits any unauthorized act in relation to
this publication may be liable to criminal
prosecution and civil claims for damage.

A CIP catalogue record for this title is
available from the British Library.

ISBN: 978-1-80439-318-5

This is a work of creative nonfiction. The events are portrayed to the best of the author's memory. While all the stories in this book are true, some names and identifying details have been changed to protect the privacy of the people involved. The opinions expressed in this book are the author's own and do not reflect the views of the publisher, author's employer, organisation, committee or other group or individual.

First Published in 2024

Olympia Publishers
Tallis House
2 Tallis Street
London
EC4Y 0AB

Printed in Great Britain

Dedication

I dedicate this book to my husband, Dragos, who always believed in me and encouraged me to fulfill my dreams.

Acknowledgements

Thank you to my husband, Dragos, for helping me write this book as well as being its first critic. Finding and being connected to someone who fully accepts you for who and what you are is a beautiful gift. For that I also want to thank you. Thank you to my parents as well – loving and supportive beings who cheerlead me at every step of my way. I can't, of course, forget here about my friends – big thank you for being part of my life despite difficulties. I would also like to thank Olympia Publishers for giving me this chance to make my dream come true. I will always be very grateful for that. And last, but not least, I wish to thank my clients who gave me a great privilege to be part of their healing journeys – it's truly a great honor.

I remember that from an early age it was important for me to make other people happy. I liked to listen and learn from the stories of others. I was a curious child — there is a saying a lot of us heard at some point *"an old soul in a young body"* – that was me (and I guess still am). Very often I heard statements like *"what a perfect child", "she is so polite and obedient; she is a great student – anyone would want such a child."* As you can imagine, this attitude helped me achieve many goals in life, but at the same time it was also destructive in consequences. Unknowingly, I began to develop perfectionism into a super strength that lowered and gradually destroyed my self-esteem and self-worth over the years.

I cannot say that there was one turning point in my life that influenced my difficulties in later years. Over the years, I came to the conclusion that there were several factors, at different stages of my life contributing to my later struggles: alcoholism in the family, my parents' divorce, death of a very close person, great sense of loss, toxic relationships, long-term illness, expectations of others not only to achieve success that they may not have been able to achieve but also to be/live in a certain way, my tendency to please others.

This book is an attempt to tell a story that may help to change some stereotypes about professionals working in the psychotherapy field. I am hoping that perhaps it will show that psychotherapists, psychologists and mental health workers are also only people who sometimes err and make unhealthy decisions in life. That they are not free from life's difficulties and problems, that they also have the right to make mistakes, lose their way, and that they carry their backpacks of experiences, which can then be helpful in their work with others. This is also a story about a woman who suffered over the years with her own identity and wanted to change her inner narrative. This is a story about a woman whose desire was to re-write her life script and find a meaning in her traumatic experiences. This book is for everyone who struggles with self-worth, body image, has experienced trauma or had abusive, toxic, co-dependent relationships. This is a book for everyone who finds it difficult to find themselves again, experienced loss of identity and grief not only when someone significant to them died but also loss of hope in others, in life, in themselves.

We all have unique stories to tell, here is mine. I was wondering for a long time whether this story would have any value, but it is not for me to judge. Are you ready to step in into my journey? Let's go then.

"Good decisions are the result of experience, and experience is gained by making wrong decisions." (Mark Twain)

CHAPTER 1

EARLY YEARS, SO HOW IT ALL BEGAN

I.
I was born in post-communist Poland in 1989. It was a breakthrough year because it was in 1989 that the communist regime was officially overthrown and democracy took its place. I don't remember much from that period (as you can imagine), except that people had money but nothing to spend it on – the shelves in the shops were empty, access to food was limited. People were queuing for ages to buy basic groceries and necessities. The basic human needs were not being met which, of course, changed with time passing by.

When I came into this world, my grandfather was a wealthy man with strong influences in my home town, so my family and I had a pretty comfortable life. Both of my parents worked, so I spent a lot of time with my grandmother, who was beloved to me, funny, warm and safe. She became my second mother and a role model to look up to. The way she was shaped many of my attitudes in adult life. When she died unexpectedly of a stroke when I was fourteen, it was a very difficult experience for me – but I'll tell you all about that a bit later.

My childhood was generally safe, full of joy, good – with a few exceptions, I guess. I studied at a private art school until I was thirteen. My grandfather was the owner of this school – from the perspective of time I can say that he showed many traits of a narcissistic personality which, of course, influenced all of the family members. He could be generous, helpful, gallant as well as arrogant, imperious, critical and despotic. All activities were aimed at some profit. He made most of the decisions regarding how my education will look like – he was definitely the head of the family. I remember very clearly his trips around the world, he was so proud of them. He always brought back a souvenir for everyone, spent hours sharing his memories from a visited country and emphasized how well he knew how to adapt in each of the countries. I was fascinated by his travels, his adventures, his experiences with other cultures – it felt like in the books I used to love reading so much! Whenever he told his adventures, I sat on his lap, my eyes were wide open, my face fully focused, and I listened carefully to what he was sharing. After each time he told his stories, I decided over and over again that I would also travel, gain these unique experiences. It took a long time for this resolution to start being fulfilled in my adult life.

 I was the best student at school. My life revolved around dancing, drawing, playing the piano, music and art competitions. To an outsider, this description may seem like a dream, but for me it was not. I think what I remember the most is the inner pressure to be the best – because if you are the best, you are noticed, praised, important, loved, right? That's how I felt then. Over the years, I was never short of comparing myself with other members of my family, which, of course, only pushed me to be even better – I didn't want to have any competition in being "the best" (and for the most part of my life I didn't). It's probably easy to see here that I was already struggling with perfectionism back then. Achievements and distinctions became strong foundation of my worth. I have never been praised for simply being only always for what I have earned, accomplished, won. Love became something conditioned, not unconditional. Let's stop here for a little longer and explore perfectionism, shall we? Perfectionism is not a homogeneous phenomenon. It can have two varieties –

one that is constructive, supportive to good adaptation to life (adaptive) and the other that hinders satisfactory functioning (maladaptive). Setting the bar high is a common feature of both types of perfectionism. In adaptive perfectionism, however, the standard is under our control. We can change it and modify it depending on the achieved results; we can opt out of it if we choose to do so. We accept our own mistakes as they are perceived as an opportunity to learn, develop and grow. We can set realistic priorities and take particular care of the most important things, and do less important things less carefully. In the maladaptive form of perfectionism, however, the standard is our master. We set ourselves unrealistic and impossible to achieve goals. We take care of every single detail because we don't know how to prioritize. We treat a minor mistake as a failure because we think in "all or nothing" ("black and white") terms. Only one hundred per cent execution – so our "everything" is acceptable, the rest falls into the category of "nothing" and is not important. The consequence of this form of perfectionism is that we cannot feel good about ourselves. We condemn ourselves to sadness, anger, fatigue and other unpleasant emotional states.

So, what contributes to perfectionism development? Well, perfectionism often develops as a result of the clash between a child's personality traits and the influences from the environment he lives in. Higher predisposition to perfectionism can be observed in intelligent, fearful, sensitive to feedback, and showing a great need for approval children. When it comes to environmental influences, the most important ones are, of course, the influences of a child's caretakers. The first situation in which maladaptive perfectionism can develop is when showing approval to the child only in the context of his particular achievements, and not in relation to his other qualities such as attitude toward people, sensitivity, diligence, creativity (as I've mentioned earlier that was my case pretty much). As a result, conditional self-esteem/self-worth develops. A child feels valuable when he is successful and worthless when he fails to be the best. So, he strives for perfection to just not to feel worthless. There is also another scenario worth mentioning here and that is when the child is punished for not achieving success (by, for example, inflicting shame, humiliation, and comparison to others). Sometimes achievements are the only way to get the attention or a way to control chaos in a child's home. Therefore, perfectionist tendencies become a defense mechanism to prevent further harm or to regain a sense of control. Parental fearfulness and fear of being imperfect may also contribute to the perfectionism development. Such parents protect the child excessively from making mistakes – they will write essays for them, check homework, and do anything is required to mask imperfection (that was also present in my family but toward another family member, not me). Finally, children of perfectionist parents can become perfectionists themselves by observing and duplicating their parents' behaviors.

Of course, at the time, I had no idea that this way of thinking, functioning, being was taking shape in me. I discovered it many years later.

II.
Remembering myself from childhood years, I can say with a smile on my face, that I was a moody child – my parents called me "grimace". I wasn't fat but definitely a chubby child – I always ate whatever was given to me; the term "pear" (that was how my dad used to facetiously call me; he stopped in my late teens) stayed with me for many years and it partly influenced my relationship with my body later on. I didn't care about my body-image back then – I liked to eat and I liked being praised. When

I did not get what I wanted, I was offended and showed everybody that I was unhappy with my "grumpy mood". I think it is worth mentioning here other characteristics of my childhood self: I was also docile, I did not rebel, I met the expectations of others, curious, brave, open, expressive, artistic, explorative, sociable, conscientious and hardworking, I liked to learn. I was the "perfect kid" (now I can see that I worked quite systematically and hard for this title and wanted to be sure I'd keep it for as long as possible to my own detriment). I was liked in and out of school; I had a lot of friends. I always had the best toys, and was the first one, in my neighborhood, to own a computer (I was almost a teenager then). Yes... I grew up in an age without cell phones, internet, computers, or social platforms. After school, all the kids in the neighborhood (including me, of course) were outside, playing games we created ourselves. We ate fruits from the trees we climbed. Parents shouted from the windows to come back home for dinner. As I recall those times, sometimes I have the impression that it was easier in the past. Reality seemed simpler, more direct and tangible. But probably every generation has similar feelings.

Let's explore then a bit more the first and most influential people in my early years – my parents. They were great and ideal (at least that's how I perceived them as a child). As an adult I've stopped idealizing them and started to realize how many of their own struggles they had to battle over the years and how much their struggles unintentionally shaped me. My mother was an Adult Child of an Alcoholic (ACA). To explain what this term means, I would like to use the definition proposed by Zofia Sobolewska-Mellibruda, who defines it as follows: *"ACA is: (...) a set of fixed personality patterns of psychosocial functioning, developed in childhood in a family with alcohol addiction. ACA syndrome creates difficulty for a person to adequately, directly maintain contact with the present due to being psychologically stuck in traumatic past. This results in experiencing and interpreting present events and relationships through the prism of painful childhood experiences. These distortions are not realized by ACA. These schemas are destructive and cause many disorders for a person in contact with self and other people, especially with those with who a person is in close relationships."* Jerzy Mellibruda draws attention to the frequent occurrences of specific unhelpful patterns in people with ACA syndrome. Their manifestations can be observed in four areas:

1. Relationship with self:
    - ∞ fear of losing our own identity/"true self" in intimate relationships,
    - ∞ low self-esteem, self-worth issues and negative attitude toward oneself,
    - ∞ fear of losing control,
    - ∞ feeling guilty when doing something for oneself,
    - ∞ difficulties in experiencing and offering self-appreciation,
    - ∞ feeling inner compulsion to be a brave person and not allowing self to have moments of weakness,
    - ∞ persistent search for approval and confirmation of self-worth by others,
    - ∞ fear of loss,
    - ∞ defensive denial of negative facts about the reality,
    - ∞ fear of positive expectations,
    - ∞ extreme propensity to take over responsibility or avoid it;

2. Relationships with other people:
    - ∞ fear of rejection,
    - ∞ deficits in the ability to harmoniously develop and deepen relationships with others,

- ∞ fear of exposing one's own unattractiveness,
- ∞ excessive sense of loyalty,
- ∞ low level of trust in others,
- ∞ the difficulty of distinguishing pity from love,
- ∞ feeling different and isolated from other people,
- ∞ difficulties in cooperating with others and a tendency to perform difficult tasks on our own;

3. Emotional life:
- ∞ low level of ability to relax and play,
- ∞ susceptibility to emotional injury,
- ∞ fear of showing own feelings,
- ∞ fear of conflict and showing anger,
- ∞ suffering associated with residual sadness,
- ∞ fear of experiencing feelings,
- ∞ impulsive behaviors and reactions;

4. Way of life:
- ∞ difficulties in finishing/ending what they started (tasks, relationships etc.)
- ∞ overreacting to changes that cannot be controlled,
- ∞ uncertainty about normality,
- ∞ experiencing life from the position of a "victim",
- ∞ black and white vision of the world especially in difficult situations,
- ∞ willingness to lie in situations where it would be easy to tell the truth,
- ∞ willingness to remain in difficult situations longer than others, regardless of personal costs,
- ∞ readiness to find satisfaction in crises and chaos rather than in a peaceful and stable life,

- ∞ tendency to addictions and compulsory activities,
- ∞ susceptibility to psychosomatic symptoms.

The symptoms of the ACA syndrome listed above do not exhaust the specifics of this kind of destructive adaptation in difficult situations. It's worth remembering that, apart from the features of ACA, people growing up in dysfunctional families may also experience: anxiety, depression, personality disorders, adaptive issues, eating disorders and addiction. Of course, my mother did not show all of these difficulties, but most of them for sure. In later years, she underwent individual as well as group therapy and freed herself from these patterns.

    My dad, on the other hand, was a child in the body of an adult – our personal Peter Pan. He was a colorful, alluring, go-getting character – a very attractive and confident person. People loved being around him and his ideas because they were fresh, original and without words like "must" or "should". He was always available and ready for some fun; his duties didn't "pull him down". He paid attention to his appearance and was aware of his attractiveness and charisma. He inherited the mania for superiority to some extent from his father. He was a womanizer big time. There was a lot of contradiction in him as he could be hard-working, responsible, focused on his business and how to improve our lives. Despite my parents' psychological challenges, as a child I felt loved, encouraged and supported by them. I remember they were both very social. They liked to see friends and family on regular basis, had fun, they loved dancing (both very good at it). Alcohol was presented in my upbringing as something associated with fun, laughter and sociability. I was taught many valuable skills, including how to respect own and others' property, how to be frugal and dispose of money wisely, be respectful of others, how to be a helpful, kind and a good little human. They both had quite strong personalities that contributed to frequent arguments and conflicts between them. I think I will never forget those evenings when I was already lying in bed, crying, because I heard their screams from the other room – they were never physical, they also never argued in front of me. So many mournful nights. I felt very lonely, confused, lost, sad in those moments as I did not fully understand what was happening. They never talked to me about their problems because why would they? I suspect they wanted to protect me. I never shared with them about hearing their arguments and fights. We were all bounded by a conspiracy of silence, pretending that nothing ever happened. I was holding up the illusion they had created. It was as if my family were creating two parallel realities: during the day we were a loving family, at night there was no family.

III.

I do not remember exactly how old I was, but it must have been in the first years of primary school, so I must have been about six or seven years old. It was the first time that I was sexually abused. He was a family member several years older than me. The first bad touch in my life. I remember being touched where I didn't want to be. I was asked to touch him in his intimate places – I refused every time. I was lying as stiff as a log, in a state of utter numbness, staring at the ceiling, hardly breathing, and waiting for it to end. I didn't understand why it was so important to this "boy", why his body reacted how it did – I was just a little girl after all. But even then, a part of me was disgusted and felt that all of this was not right, that it shouldn't have happened. Abuse happened several times; I was paid for my silence and threatened that if I told someone about it, people would say that I was a liar.

That nobody would believe me and he will deny it anyway. Since then, I tried my best not to be left alone with him to avoid the abuse as even a thought of it made me want to vomit. I didn't want to be touched like that, but I didn't quite know why, I just didn't like it. I didn't reveal this secret; my mind quickly and efficiently pushed these experiences into the deep recesses of my unconscious. It was only many years later that I told to my husband and to my therapist about it. Trauma is often seen as a mental problem, and traumatized people often are unable to feel or accept sympathy. Their emotions have been displaced, and the reptilian brain comes to the fore, triggering primary defense mechanisms. Trauma is not always related to external events that directly caused mental or physical pain. Trauma is a response to a painful experience by closing yourself to it in order to survive. It arises when a person is unable to release blocked energy or to follow the physical reactions and emotions that are a natural response to being hurt. In a state of excessive stress (traumatic event), there is a switch from the "learning brain" mode to the "survival brain" mode. When a child (even unknowingly) feels threatened, his brain switches to one of five alarm modes:

∞ Fighting – the child is entering over-aroused state of being. Here we can observe trouble concentrating and understanding what is said to the child. The child can be aggressive and rebel. The child fights for its survival.

∞ Flight – it manifests by timidity and withdrawal of a child (physically running away or emotional withdrawal). A child presents difficulty in calming own emotions, memory is affected and retention of information as well. A child has problems with learning and self-esteem.

∞ Freeze – in nature, when an animal can't fight a predator and knows it won't escape from a life threatening situation its brain triggers its ultimate defense mechanism – freezing. The animal collapses and "plays dead" in the hope that its predator will lose its interest and leave. The child in freeze mode is avoidant and withdrawn, struggles with motivation, feels chronically tired, lethargic, or restless.

∞ Submit – an important part of this mode is shame; shame is an emotion that is activated every time we think that we have broken a social norm. Shame is an extremely important emotion that also helps to minimize harm and damage. Interestingly, shame plays a very important developmental role, because the implication of shame helps inhibit certain behaviors (for example: when a small child picks up a dangerous object, the parent, by activating shame, causes the child to put the item down – what it is important here is that an adult can take the shame away by, for example, hugging the child immediately after activating the shame – an adult is "repairing" the emotional state of the child; in the case of trauma, the shame is not repaired but repeated over and over again).

∞ Attach (cry for help) – attach is one of the survival mechanisms too. Clinging, embracing, grasping is used by the child to regulate the tension associated with stress. As a child is not able to regulate his emotional states on his own, he needs the parent's intervention to help him to do so. In adulthood, people in this mode seek comfort at all costs and excessive closeness with others, have difficulties with making their own decisions, there is a difficulty with self-regulation, which can causes dependence on others.

In any of the survival modes, we can lose the ability to remember and learn; we can lose our self-esteem and self-worth. When the brain feels threatened it turns off all the higher functions of the prefrontal cortex, which include: language, reflective thinking (under stress a lot of people are simply unable to speak, their mouths are open but the words are just not coming out), creative thinking, empathy, mathematical abilities, self-control, strong will, patience and much more as the main focus is elsewhere – the brain focuses on just surviving. When going through a traumatic event, a child has difficulty concentrating and remembering. He/she can easily "turn off" or become impulsive. A child may get stuck in a state of high (fight) or too little agitation (flight, freeze) for a short time, months or even years. Children who are chronically "mind-boggling" or hyperactive are in no way "weaker" or rude. It also doesn't mean that they aren't trying hard enough. They simply experience excessive stress in their everyday lives or, in other words, they are being re-triggered on a frequent basis. I think it is important to keep in mind that there are no stupid children, unfit or naughty children. There are only children whose limbic systems are overly reactive and one of the reasons for that might be that they never processed their traumatic experiences.

In retrospect, I can say that this period of my childhood was a turning point for me when it comes to my later relationship to sex, relationship with the body and choosing emotionally unavailable partners. I was in freeze mode for years without realizing it. My trauma was unprocessed on a somatic level for twenty-five years.

IV.

Every summer, my parents took me to my grandparents, who lived more than three hundred kilometers from my home city. I stayed there for the entire two months (in Poland, children have their summer holidays in July and August). For many years I loved going there – I had a lot of friends, days were filled with plays and games, living a stress-free life really well to some degree. I was very popular, had my first experiences of holding hands with boys, even a kiss on the cheek. I didn't cause any troubles to my grandparents. I did what I was told – always in the role of the "perfect child". My grandparents' place was the place where for the first time I encountered addiction and co-dependency in their worse forms. My grandfather was an active alcoholic, and my grandmother was co-dependent on him and his addiction. Most of my aunts and uncles drank, and their drinking was different from the drinking I knew from back home. There was no laughter, no fun, no dancing, no music, no social aspect. For the first time, I watched people change when drunk. I'm sure you have heard the story of Doctor Jekyll and Mr. Hyde? That's what happened with my family members – they changed from quiet, hard-working, somewhat grounded into aggressive, violent, loud, furious, raging, dysfunctional people. I felt fearful to be around them when they were in that drunken state. I don't remember how many times my drunken grandfather yelled at me that I was a whore, that I was looking for a sponsor and that I would go wherever I could to fuck; that I'm a worthless rag. I've also heard comments about my physical appearance quite frequently. *"You could be thinner", "You should eat less", "Dress like a girl, look at yourself!"* I was a tomboy, so what? I did what boys do, I dressed like a boy, I even had a haircut like a boy, I didn't like dresses, I preferred cars to dolls, etc. I was young, wild and free as a child is supposed to be. I have to admit one thing – he never raised his hand to me, unfortunately other family members were not so lucky. So, I guess I could consider myself lucky, right? When I write about all of this as an adult, I know now that we've all dealt with psychological abuse and, obviously, alcohol addiction. Let me tell you here a little bit more about both of these. If we want to talk about alcohol addiction, first of all we need to think about what addiction in general is. What is this phenomenon characterized by, what changes in behaviors can occur in addicts, what stages addiction includes and what kind of social consequences of this phenomenon are. Gabor Maté says, *"addiction is manifested in any behavior that a person craves, finds temporary relief or pleasure in but suffers negative consequences as a result of, and yet has difficulty giving up."* The most general division that can be used in the case of addiction is: physiological and psychological. When looking at physiological addiction, we are dealing with an increase in tolerance level of the body to a substance of choice, which leads to the emergence of an addiction – the person's body consumes repetitively a given substance and becomes addicted (dependent) to it, which means that a person must constantly supply a specific substance to the body, and in case of stopping, the body experiences withdrawal symptoms. Examples of withdrawal symptoms can include: nausea, sweating, trembling limbs. In some cases, the withdrawal symptoms may be so severe that they lead to the person's death. Psychological addiction, on the other hand, is understood as the emergence of a very strong desire to take a substance of choice. This is due to the fact that the user finds the consumption of a given substance exceptionally attractive and pleasant. Thanks to the development of an unrestrained desire to take a given substance, the functioning of an individual changes dramatically – the person and his life begin to focus on the use of an addictive substance, which in consequence lowers the level of social functioning. In connection with physiological dependence, the individual, due to the increasing tolerance of the organism, must, over time, increase the doses of the delivered substance to obtain a desirable effect (based on: Zimbardo, Gerrig., 2008). Since the phenomenon of addiction is such a broad concept, how can we say that a person

is addicted? There are many symptoms that can indicate this. Some factors will only appear in relation to a specific measure. However, the symptoms that characterize all addictions and occur in each of them are:
- ∞ an individual's behavior quickly becomes habitual;
- ∞ behavior becomes regular, frequent and stereotyped;
- ∞ there is an inability to stop the behavior;
- ∞ the individual spends a significant amount of time on drinking, using, etc.;
- ∞ problems arise from it (including professional, family, health, emotional, financial);
- ∞ there is an internal compulsion to perform a given activity;
- ∞ there is a presence of withdrawal symptoms after an attempt to stop (based on: Mellibruda, 2012).

Addiction is a very destructive phenomenon not only for the individual, but also for his immediate environment. The longer a person remains in addiction, the worse its effects can get. What many addicts do not know (or don't want to acknowledge) is that their disease also affects those who live with them. Many facts are denied by them – it is one of the defensive mechanisms presented among addicts. Let's move now from generic exploration of addiction and focus purely on alcoholism. The concept of alcoholism was introduced in 1849 by Magnus Huss. In 1952, Czech doctor Elvin Morton Jellinek, introduced the first phases division in alcoholism (The Jellinek Curve). He distinguished the following:
- ∞ introductory phase (or pre-alcoholic stage) – this is the first phase of alcoholism and may last from several months to several years, even. It is very often referred to in the literature as the social drinking stage. The most significant characteristics of this phase are the discovery

by the drinker that alcohol not only provides pleasure, but also reduces the negative emotional states from different experiences. In this phase, the body's tolerance to alcohol changes as well (I am sure you have heard that someone had a "strong head" to drink… well now you know why; I was in that phase but you will find out more about it later on);

∞ warning phase – second stage in which the drinker starts to experience memory gaps related to his drinking behaviors. Here we also observe increase in initiating meetings in order to drink. After having a drink, the person becomes more sociable, the so-called "life and soul of the party" and his well-being improves to a large extent (for a short while of course). Due to the change in tolerance level, the doses of alcohol increase, which causes drunkenness and hangover drinking (the so-called "wedge" is a term used by addicts – having a drink the next morning to reduce hangover basically), there is also drinking secretly, in solitude present here (my grandfather was definitely a loner when it came to him getting smashed);

∞ critical phase – this is the third phase of the alcoholism, in which the individual stops controlling their drinking. There are various issues between them and their families, environment, work, health, but also conflicts with the law (not always though). The person neglects his outward appearance, feels guilty about drinking, and makes numerous excuses for his drinking. There is also an abstinence syndrome – a person drinks in binges that are intertwined with momentary moments of complete abstinence. The level of aggressiveness in the drinker also increases, and false promises are made to stop drinking (very observable pattern in my grandfather's functioning);

∞ chronic phase - this is the last phase distinguished by Jellinek. At this stage of the addiction, the drinker uses many days of binge drinking, family ties are broken, alcoholic psychosis, social degradation, and theft of alcohol appear. There is a significant decrease in the body's tolerance to alcohol. Alcohol becomes the most important and the only life goal to the addicted person. If the above phase is not interrupted, it may result in the death of the drinker (Jellinek, 1952 after: Mellibruda J., Sobolewska-Mellibruda Z. 2006). My grandfather has been in this stage for a long time now and I don't think he will ever stop his self-destruction.

Each of the above phases has different consequences that the drinker must confront sooner or later. The sooner the person realizes that she/he has a problem with alcohol the easier and faster she/he will be able to break free from alcohol addiction.

Since then, different stages in addiction development have been distinguished. One of the more useful classifications is that of the World Health Organization's Committee of Experts on Alcoholism presents. The most commonly used definition of alcoholism today is one presented by the ICD-10 (F10 – mental and behavioral disorders caused by alcohol use): "*A cluster of behavioral, cognitive, and physiological phenomena that develop after repeated substance use and that typically include a strong desire to take the drug, difficulties in controlling its use, persisting in its use despite harmful consequences, a higher priority given to drug use than to other activities and obligations, increased tolerance, and sometimes a physical withdrawal state.*

The dependence syndrome may be present for a specific psychoactive substance (e.g. tobacco, alcohol, or diazepam), for a class of substances (e.g. opioid drugs), or for a wider range of pharmacologically different psychoactive substances" (ICD-10, 2019). In order to be completely sure of the accuracy of the diagnosis of alcoholism, ICD-10 provides diagnostic criteria, of which at least three must be present to talk about alcohol dependence. These are:

1. *"a strong desire to take a substance or experience a feeling of compulsion to take it;*

2. *difficulties in controlling behaviors around substance use, initiation, termination or the amount;*

3. *physiological withdrawal symptoms occurring after discontinuation or reduction of the intake of the substance, in the form of a substance-specific withdrawal syndrome;*

4. *establishing tolerance, namely increasing doses are needed to produce the effects previously caused by lower doses;*

5. *because of taking psychoactive substances – increasing neglect of alternative sources of pleasure or interests, increased amount of time spent on acquiring or taking a substance or reversing the consequences of its action;*

6. *substance use continues despite clear evidence of overtly harmful consequences, such as liver damage due to heavy drinking, depressed mood states due to periods of heavy substance use, or drug-induced cognitive impairment."* (ICD-10, 2019).

The above definition, together with the diagnostic criteria, is the most extensive definition in the literature. In my humble opinion, it shows exactly all the aspects that are significant to be taken into account when diagnosing a person addicted to alcohol. A person addicted to alcohol cannot admit to oneself that he is an alcoholic. Most often he denies his addiction, but how is that this particular person becomes addicted? After all, not everyone who drinks is addicted, right? According to Wiktor Osiatyński, alcoholism is more than just a disease. He perceives the phenomenon of addiction as a lack of certain social skills *"related to self-knowledge, behavioral control, shaping and expressing feelings, as well as establishing interpersonal relationships"* (Osiatyński, 2007), but also points out that not every person who does not have these important skills will become addicted to alcohol. However, every alcoholic does not actually have these skills and must learn them in order to stay sober in their recovery. So what does an addicted person look like from a clinical point of view? What criteria were adopted? Let me try to explore this aspect below.

If we want to show the functioning of an addicted person as best as possible, it would be beneficial to, first of all, focus on the pathological mechanisms that coexist with alcoholism. Jerzy Mellibruda (2002) points out some very interesting ones:

∞ compulsive emotional regulation mechanism – alcoholics have a disturbed emotional life as a result of their drinking and each emotional state, no matter what source it comes from, is perceived by them as a strong need to drink (receiving "bad news" is a good reason to drink as well as receiving "good news"). This mechanism is aimed at regulating unpleasant emotions (they will not say "no" to alcohol if they experienced some pleasurable emotions too) with alcohol. Addicts do not try to change the situation or circumstances that cause their unpleasant states. They look for the relief in their suffering that alcohol provides (they drink to numb their emotions). Because of the changing tolerance level to alcohol, drinkers also experience various ailments, not only mental, but also physical, which results in the appearance of anxiety, depression, agitation and irritation. The desire to neutralize ailments as quickly as possible and experience a sense of calmness is known as the so-called alcohol craving;

∞ illusion and denial mechanism – this mechanism arises as a result of a dissonance created by the confrontation of two contradictory information – on the one hand, the drinker is aware of the negative effects of consuming large amounts of alcohol, and on the other hand, the positive effects of drinking result in denial of the negative effects of alcohol abuse. The person addicted to alcohol builds a system of coherent beliefs about the subjective vision of life that is not confirmed in the real world. In flashes of consciousness, an alcoholic confronted with the real effects of destructive alcohol consumption allows himself to think about stopping drinking. Through this experience, however, he feels negative and unpleasant emotional states again, which results in their drinking and activating compulsive emotional regulation mechanisms;

∞ mechanism of distraction and split self – this mechanism concerns the structure of self which is contained in the human personality and causes impairment of behavior control and the inability to make decisions by alcoholics. An addict with a split self does not have an integrated sense of individuality and consistency. This leads to the creation of two opposing poles in the personality of the addicted person – on the one hand, false and illusionistic visions of their own merits, competences, and strengths arise, and on the other hand, a negative feeling of their own failures, inappropriate behaviors, and losses incurred as a result of their addiction. These two contradictory poles become the most dominant internal states experienced by alcoholics (Mellibruda, 2002).

The above mechanisms shape the overall attitudes and the functioning of the alcoholic. Over time, distorted beliefs and contradictory judgements about oneself and others deepen and destroy the personal, family, and social life of the addicted person. The effects of drinking alcohol centralize the alcoholic's behaviors around his addiction – alcohol consumption becomes his top priority and the most important life goal to be met each day. Addicts become obsessed with drinking – they stop focusing on themselves because something else has become more valuable and precious to them. They neglect their health, stop controlling their behaviors, start to separate from people.

Moving on slightly from addiction let me tell you now a little something about psychological abuse we as a family experienced. We usually have no problems recognizing physical violence. Using physical violence causes pain and often leaves visible traces in the form of wounds, fractures and bruises. Physical violence can be recognized easier, quicker, is more obvious. Psychological abuse, however, is more problematic. Often, the victims of psychological abuse do not know that they are dealing with it. Nor is it always known how to prove psychological abuse as the traces of it are not obvious. Psychological abuse is such a form of interaction with another person that makes them feel bad. All insults, humiliation, blackmail, threats and manipulations are considered psychological abuse. Over time, they take a recurring form and become more intense. Although psychological abuse does not leave any physical marks, it has serious mental consequences for the victims and their environment. Victims of this form of abuse are more likely to suffer from depression, experience anxiety, and often attempt suicide. They have significant self-esteem and self-worth issues. If children become victims of psychological abuse, it may affect their emotional and intellectual development. For adults, psychological abuse has an apparent effect in changing their behaviors. People who experienced psychological abuse can become withdrawn, passive, silent and isolate themselves from others. They often blame themselves for the abuse, and they are coming to the conclusion that because of some of their behaviors they deserved such a "treatment". In this way, the victim formulates an attached and dependent relationship with their perpetrator. Sometimes there are attempts to escape from reality by alcohol, drugs and other addictive substances or behaviors. Psychological abuse can take many different forms. They are often individual in nature, but there are also a few repetitive behaviors. Some of them are:

- ∞ disrespect toward the victims, which is manifested, for example, by disregarding their work, not taking into account their opinions, etc.; disrespectful behaviors are often accentuated in the presence of third parties;
- ∞ limiting the victim's contacts with other people, which may take the form of controlling their correspondence and conversations, cutting them off from the relations with family and friends;
- ∞ morbid jealousy, accusations of or willingness to betrayal, finding its hallmarks in every action toward third parties;
- ∞ threats of physical aggression, hitting walls, countertops, slamming doors, destroying things (throwing plates, etc.);

∞ verbal aggression, screams, quarrels, insults – but also persistent silence ("silent treatment").

These types of behaviors are very often a symptom of psychological violence, but everyone has moments of weakness in which they behave inappropriately so it is important to be mindful and not label a singular incident e.g. when we had an argument with our partner and they raised their voice and that's not their usual way of dealing with conflict. Psychological abuse is the result of long-term violence that is characterized by some internal organization. As mentioned earlier, the aggressor tries to isolate his/her victim by limiting or breaking their contacts with the outside world. The abuser also tries to cut off the victim from any activities that would be appreciated by others – such as work or hobbies. In this way, the aggressor makes his/her victim dependent on oneself. He then manipulates the victim in such a way that she begins to blame herself for the psychological abuse that has occurred. For the manipulation purposes, the abuser can pretend to be a victim as well, for example, uses crying to arouse pity. Apart from the violent episodes, there are times when the abuser tries to be nice and charming. The victim begins to suspect that they are responsible for any negative situations themselves, which of course is only the result of manipulation.

    My grandfather was the only person in my life I truly hated for a long time. For many years I had not revealed to my parents what happened during the summer holidays. I am sure my mother knew to some degree as she experienced all of it herself in her childhood (from what she told me later on it was even worse back then). Maybe she hoped that he has changed to some degree over the years? When I turned fourteen and entered a public school (which of course was very bluntly judged and criticized by my "wealthy, perfect" family) I never went for summer holidays there ever again… and I haven't seen my alcoholic grandfather for over thirteen years.

V.
Somewhere in between all these family experiences my parents divorced – I was eleven at the time. From an early age, I was very closely attached to my dad. He was always funny, gave me more freedom in doing different things, pampered me, treated me like his little princess, was my best friend (and still is). As mentioned before, he was my private Peter Pan. I am not saying that I was not close to my mother, because I was, but it was my mother who was more demanding, set the rules and household duties, imposed punishments, and enforced the consequences. She was more of a responsible, authoritarian parent. She was also a parent who screamed and expressed anger when she was sad, nervous, anxious, angry, afraid, feeling helpless, powerless, scared. So basically, the majority of difficult emotions she expressed through anger. Now, I understand that anger was the most acceptable emotion in her childhood household. I often work with anger with my clients and I introduce a metaphor of an iceberg to demonstrate how we can mask different emotions behind it. Imagine that the top of the iceberg is anger – that is what we see, that is what stands out from the water. But if we were to dive in and see the invisible part of the iceberg we may discover: fear, hurt, disappointment, anxiety, depression, stress, loneliness, embarrassment, shame, tiredness, grief, insecurity, guilt, jealousy, powerlessness, helplessness, contempt and many other emotions we are afraid to express openly. Anger can act like a very powerful mask protecting us from further damage. Anger can feel powerful, strong, and invincible. And my mother wore

such a mask for a long time. She and I stayed in the family home after their divorce; my dad moved out which I found extremely challenging. We were still close, we still spent a lot of time together, but somewhere inside I felt a limitation of time we had together. During this time, my mother underwent addiction treatment (unfortunately, I don't remember much from the period when she was in the rehab; I only remember that my father took me there once to visit her – I came back from there thinking what a depressing place it was and how destroyed were the people there) and freed herself from alcohol addiction. She also undertook individual and group psychotherapy and addressed her deeply rooted issues. She has now been sober for twenty-three years – such a great achievement! I am very proud of her. In the Alcoholic Anonymous (A.A.) fellowship (is a voluntary, self-help group of people addicted to alcohol or other addictive substances/behaviors, created in order to maintain their own sobriety and support other alcoholics/addicts in achieving/maintaining sobriety. The foundation of AA's philosophy is the Twelve Steps), she met my brother's father, with whom she broke up eleven years later. She is currently happily married to a very cool guy she met in A.A. My brother has a great bond with him. A few years after the divorce, my dad moved to England (he is also happily married now and has twin boys), where I started going on summer holidays every year.

Divorce in a family system can be one of the most difficult and painful events in spouses and their children's lives. Children, due to their emotional immaturity, dependence on parents, strong need to feel safe and vulnerable, experience divorce more strongly than adults. That is why it is so important that children receive adequate support during this challenging process (my parents took really good care of that; I sometimes say *"they divorced with class and dignity"*). For the first time in a long while they really came together and agreed, without conflict, how they would divide their goods so it would benefit me and my development as well as maintain a sense of stability. I didn't have to go to court or be involved in the process in any way, shape or form. But not every child experiences this process smoothly. So, what does divorce actually mean to a child? What kind of emotional and developmental consequences the child may face because his/her family system is breaking apart? Well, let me share with you a bit more about this. First of all, it is worth mentioning that children from families in which their parents constantly argue, fight or remain silent experience much greater emotional problems than those in which their parents have decided to part ways. More often in families where there are constant quarrels and arguments, there is more hatred present than love. In such situations, children can internalize and mirror their parents' feelings of hostility and anger. The stress associated with a permanently tense atmosphere at home can cause psychosomatic (physical symptoms caused by mental factors e.g. emotional distress, internal conflict) issues in a child. Therefore, deciding to divorce often turns out to be a constructive solution in comparison to functioning together in a destructive family system. The breakup itself is almost always preceded by various pre-divorce conflicts observed by the children. The parents' break-up and their conflicts may cause the loss of sense of security and lower self-esteem in a child. The child may experience helplessness and powerlessness because he or she cannot influence the parents' decisions. There may also be helplessness, guilt and anxiety over the need to choose between a father and a mother. Children can feel emotional burden due to being drawn into their arguments and expectation from parents to take sides. Parents, often unknowingly, draw their children over to "their side" and evoke negative feelings toward the other parent. The child then experiences a cognitive dissonance (we can explain it as a state of mental disorientation which can occur in people who have knowledge of two different views on a given topic that are contradictory. The emergence of cognitive dissonance is when someone's thoughts about what they know, how they feel, and what needs to be done to resolve a given situation contradict each other) consisting in making a choice of a parent who "should be loved" and who "should be rejected". As a consequence, the child experiences an inner feeling of being torn apart, a lack of loyalty and being treated more like "an object to win over" by his parents. Often in adulthood, opting for one of the sides may manifest itself in depression, anxiety, guilt and shame. So every often, it can also happen that one of the parents consciously isolates himself from the child in order to protect himself from the suffering associated with separation and leaves the parent with a feeling of great loss.

Many stressful and tense situations can arise during a divorce and breakup. If parents have difficulty controlling their emotions, they can unintentionally set a negative behavioral pattern for their child. Because of that, children potentially can learn to lie, be hostile and distrust others. It is important for parents to be able to cope with their difficult emotions during this challenging process so they can be ready and prepared to support their children. There are a lot of research on this topic suggesting that children (and adults if the divorce is happening in their adulthood) who are more resistant to stress and who experience parental support adapt faster to the new family situation. So, what kind of consequences might a young person experience on the emotional level because of divorce? I allowed myself to separate different age groups here so it will perhaps be clearer to demonstrate different consequences. Let's have a closer look:

Infancy:
The child feels and empathizes very strongly on the emotional level with her parents. The first years of a child's life are particularly important in shaping his/her personality and healthy development. When at an early stage of the child's life one of the parents is missing or is replaced by a different person, unknown to the child, then a child can experience fear and loses the sense of security and stability. The departure of someone who has met all of the child's needs can result in various difficulties such as sleep problems and frequent changes in mood. Strong anxiety can be also present and most often manifested by excessive tearfulness.

Three to five years of age:
Children notice that one of the parents does not live at home, but they do not understand why. They live in the hope that it will be the same as before and that the absent parent will eventually come back. If the parents are busy resolving their conflicts or forming new relationships during this time, the child's sense of abandonment can appear. At this stage, the loss of security and uncertainty about the future can cause sleep disturbances, frequent abdominal pain and other physiological symptoms. Intensely experienced emotions may cause a return to the earlier developmental stages (for example to the stage when the child was under the care of both parents). The child may feel clingy, retreat to thumb-sucking, or bed-wetting frequently. Pre-school children often blame themselves for the departure of one of their parents and see the blame in their "bad behaviors". There may be also present some aggressive behavior toward a parent who

stayed or toward other children in social situations. Impulsive and hyperactive behaviors may also appear. Children can also experience fear and abandonment.

School age:
Children at this stage understand that parents no longer love each other and will not live together. Despite their understanding, they hope that their parents will get back together. They miss the parent who is not there anymore and blame the parent they believe broke up the marriage. Strong emotional experiences and long-term stress associated with pre-divorce conflicts and the divorce itself, and then with adapting to the new situation, often can cause some learning difficulties and educational problems for even the most gifted children. As in younger children, there may be some somatic issues experienced such as abdominal pain, headache, vomiting. Often, these issues may appear after meeting the parent who is no longer living at home as an expression of reluctance to part with him or fear that the parents will quarrel again. Children can also feel that they "should" be loyal to the parent they live with as they are afraid to lose them. They can also hide their home situation from others out of shame. The negative emotions experienced by children during their parents' divorce may lower their self-esteem and lose faith in their own abilities. There is also a disturbance in feeling secure. Some children idealize the parent they do not live with, and they discharge their anger, grief and hurt onto the parent they live with. Children are often denying that they do not see any connection between their parents' quarrels and separation. Here again, children can blame themselves and their behaviors as the reasons for the divorce.

Puberty:

As puberty for many young people is a time of emotional instability, divorce at this stage can be even more difficult to deal with. Young people already know what divorce is, but do not have to accept it anyway. A parent's need for emotional support during a divorce, caring for younger siblings, new responsibilities and social roles can overburden a teenager. On top of that, parents sometimes require the child to decide who to stay with, which can be very stressful for the child. There may be difficulties in accepting new partners by a teenager. They can feel uncomfortable, blame the parent's new partner for the breakdown of the marriage, and can be jealous. Often a young person, as a consequence of the divorce, may be distrustful of other people and fear that his/her future relationships will end up the same way. Some adolescents also try to attract attention by rebellion, destructively solving their problems through socially unacceptable behavior. They can often run away from home, truant, commit minor crimes (like shoplifting), abuse psychoactive substances, present self-aggressive behavior and might experience suicidal thoughts. Reactions to conflicts in the family often include isolating oneself, reluctance to talk about problems and being closed to any help or support. There is also a reduced motivation to learn and difficulties with concentration. Young people preparing to enter adulthood can experience abandonment on their part instead of leaving their parents. This often results in the necessity to face the adult world and to assume various roles, e.g. the confidants of their parents. You will later see that I was presenting a lot of listed emotional and behavioral patterns from "school age" and puberty stages but let's not jump ahead, shall we?

Two families, two different worlds – one family considered itself better than the others, haughty, calculated, arrogant, with a sense of power, superiority and narcissism. Every now and then able to be loving, proud, warm, supportive. Narcissistic families are like spiders that trap their children in a web of emotional suffering. In this kind of family dynamic, there will always be one person who puts his/her whims over the needs of other members, thus gaining absolute power (like in my family it was a grandfather). They use it to manipulate the rest of the family so that they are cared for, appreciated and recognized at all possible levels. People who grow up in such dysfunctional environments often say that their family looks perfect on the outside but is hell on the inside. It's not easy to get out of this situation, not at all. And while the bonds that develop in every family differ, they still share some characteristics. The biggest characteristic feature of narcissistic families is the existence of very specific but unwritten rules. These are rules that revolve around one person. They take away any rights and recognition from all other members. Only one is a true ruler of the family system. The truth about unhealthy family dynamics is often silenced by some sort of punishment e.g. extradition. In fact, when a child becomes an adult and can finally escape from a difficult childhood, he/she is labelled as a "bad child" for deciding to abandon the family (like I was for a number of years), for having the courage to break ties. When you are part of this kind of family portrait, it is not easy to get away as growing up in it involves internalizing many destructive dictates, thought patterns and ideas that have a significant impact on a child's mind. Let me tell you some other common features of narcissistic families:

- ∞ You act like your family is the best and don't tell anyone outside what's going on. Narcissistic families are very concerned about their image. In fact, they often say, *"we have no problems, we are the perfect family"* (yep, pretty

much that's the perfect mirror of my family);
- ∞ Dysfunctional parents: the role of a parent in a healthy family system is to provide safety, love, education, and emotional support to their children. In narcissistic families, children have two responsibilities: to educate and take care of their parents (that wasn't the case in my childhood but in my parents' childhoods definitely yes);
- ∞ Lack of effective communication: the most common type of communication in narcissistic families is triangulation. In other words, family members are never direct with each other and can display passive-aggressive behavior based on tension and distrust (my family never used open, honest, assertive, direct communication; "dirty bits" were treated as a family secret we were not supposed to ever talk about).

Being in an environment where emotional rules are distorted is not only unhealthy, it can also be unbearable, especially for children. When children become adults, they usually have difficulties with saying "no" to other people or do not understand that they have the right to set boundaries (definitely in my case). They also have trouble expressing their own desires and needs and making choices about what to tolerate or not (as you will see later that was very much the case in my life).

The other side of the family was full of addictions, dysfunctions, violence, lacking love, unity, connection. As we know, the family unit plays a fundamental role in a child's mental health. It is emphasized that the husband and wife (or any caretakers) are the architects of the family. Their parental skills are fundamental in how their children will develop. So what happens in a home that is dysfunctional? What is a dysfunctional family and how does it function? What kind of roles can children take in such a family system? Well, let's see.

Based on John Bradshaw, a dysfunctional family is created by a dysfunctional marriage. People with dysfunctions very often find another person who acts either at the same level or at a higher level of dysfunction. Children growing up in a dysfunctional family are innocent; they have no control over the toxic, unhealthy environment in which they grow up. They are hurt by adults on different levels: physical, emotional, psychological, and sexual. For such children, uncertainty, chaos and the instability of the environment are everyday life (due to its repetitiveness there is a high probability that these patterns will be normalized and repeated by them in their adulthood if unaddressed in therapy, for example). Children from dysfunctional homes do not receive the attention and support they need in key stages of their development. Instead, they focus on the dysfunctional behaviors of their parents. Very often they cannot show their feelings (especially anger, sadness and fear – these are considered "not allowed" emotions to express). So, in that case, what can cause family dysfunction? Let me list some of the most common contributing factors:

- physical, emotional, sexual abuse,
- addiction,
- personality disorders and other psychological problems,
- family conflicts,
- conflict between parent and child,
- religious fanaticism,
- abandonment,
- neglect.

For the family system to survive, children need to take on different roles. They do it out of love for their caretakers. Children undertake tasks that are beyond their capabilities and they work hard to maintain "balance" in the family. The roles described below serve the family, but not the children who identify with them:

- ∞ **"Hero"** – is a child who plays the role of an adult in the family. The child's job is to provide the family with self-esteem, hope, pride and success. The child takes on this role because one or both parents are emotionally unavailable or immature due to their own psychological problems. Despite the fact that the child has not gone through the full cycle of adolescence and maturation and is unable to cope with such a challenge, he plays such a role, although internally he is not prepared for it. He usually takes on various responsibilities and copes with them very well (e.g. cooking, cleaning, raising younger siblings). He is brave, composed, dedicated and ready to give up on himself for others. The extended family, friends and neighbors often look at such a child with envy, praise and admiration. Thanks to the hero, the family can feel good about themselves, because it has brought up such a responsible and successful young person;

- ∞ **"Scapegoat"** – it allows the family to distract from their real problems. The family treats the child as a kind of substitute object on which they concentrate and unload negative feelings. The scapegoat role is the opposite of the family hero. Adults perceive such a child as irresponsible and difficult, bringing troubles and problems with their behaviors. The child often performs poorly in school, uses various substances early, and falls into the so-called "bad crowd". He is usually brazen and arrogant toward caretakers. In this way, he expresses the negative emotions that family members expose him to. The scapegoat child, however, can be surprisingly similar to the family hero: he can take responsibility for what happens in the family. But the hero takes responsibility for the positive image of the family, and the scapegoat for the negative one. Children in both roles experience fear, a sense of rejection, loneliness and harm. The scapegoat also sometimes has a feeling of hatred toward the world and people who give him no chance to be good, as well as feelings of jealousy and underestimation;

∞ **"Mascot"** – the mascot child is mainly responsible for improving the mood and humor of the family. It provides a relief of tensions with laughter, jokes, and humor in an otherwise sad and frightening family environment. It often becomes a home antidote to crisis moments. Many children who develop hyperactivity simply try to relieve tension in the family by fooling around and paying attention to themselves. Parents like to show off their mascot child in front of others. At the same time, regardless of age, they treat the child as an immature person who understands little of what is happening around him. Since he is not taken too seriously by the family, he is often not informed about various matters and does not take part in decision-making processes. When a mascot has to deal with someone else's anger or rage against which adult household members are powerless, he is actually scared and tense. He very often has the feeling that if he cannot improve someone's mood, he becomes unnecessary like an abandoned, useless cuddly toy;

∞ **"The invisible child"** (sometimes also called "the child in the fog" or "the lost child") – acts as if he was not there. He often feels that it would be better if he wasn't there at all. He can take care of himself for hours. Such a child does not cause any problems with education; usually does not want anything. In social interactions the invisible child is withdrawn, sometimes considered super shy. He does everything necessary to not draw attention to himself. Sometimes he succeeds so well that he grows up feeling isolated and alone, despite the people around him. Such a child lacks basic interpersonal skills such as: establishing deep and meaningful relationships, expressing his needs or cooperating with others. At school, he clearly differs from his peers on the social skills level.

And here I was, somewhere in between these two very different worlds. Always bouncing in between, never fully identified with either side. When analyzing the above-mentioned roles later on in life, I most often identified myself with the role of a "hero", but I must admit that I often changed roles depending on a given situation. Each role is somehow useful for the child, and it was the same for me. Depending on what I needed and how I felt at the time, I chose different roles. Of course switching between roles didn't happen on a conscious level.

Reflecting over the years about my upbringing, such a rift between families had a profound effect on my core beliefs. Basic beliefs in us, humans, form knowledge about ourselves, others, and the world in which we live. The most important beliefs begin to form from an early age. They are based on our interpretations of the situations in which we participate and in our interactions with the people around us. Very often core beliefs sources are primarily from our parents, family members, older siblings, and then schoolmates, teachers, and later partners, friends – that is, generally speaking, people who are somehow important, significant and valuable to us. The child learns about the world by observing and copying what he observes in others, it allows him to learn to navigate this complicated world when he does not fully know what it is about and how it works. Due to the period in which basic beliefs are formed, they are characterized by, among other things, the fact that they take the form of simple, uncomplicated disempowering statements, for example: *"I am hopeless", "I am ugly", "others are critical", "the world is a dangerous place", "I cannot trust others", "I cannot be happy because something bad will happen."* They can also be supportive and empowering, for example: *"I am special", "I am loved", "others are helpful", "I am important", "I am beautiful", "the world is safe."* Another characteristic of core beliefs is that we take them for granted, as an automatic truth about ourselves, the world, and others – we do not question their validity or truthfulness, at least during childhood, as we do not have the resources to do so. They are deeply ingrained in our psyche and very often we are not aware of them. Imagine that they act like lenses in glasses you are wearing every day. Looking through the beliefs' prism our reality takes shapes, shades; we form our interpretations about different things. Depending on what kind of lenses we wear (what beliefs we hold), they will determine what and how we perceive the world and also how we will act in different situations. They are a kind of unique filter that automatically selects the perceived information. In other words, information selection will tend to catch information that confirms our core beliefs and omit or distort information that undermines them. In my case, some of the beliefs that I formed were like this: *"by achieving the best results and being obedient I am loved and important"*, *"I cannot trust boys"*, *"good results in school define my value"*, *"I am ugly and chubby"*, *"I have no right to make a mistake"*, *"I am not good enough"* (some characteristics of the ACA syndrome here can be observed already in me), *"I am intelligent"*, *"I have beautiful eyes"*. Of course, I was not aware of them at the time. For many years, I idealized my childhood because I was generally a happy child. What I didn't realize was that I had built up the belief that *"love was conditional"* and that my self-esteem is conditioned by external factors (achievements, results, how others perceive me, and so on). My locus of self-worth was external which means that one "bad" action or decision and it crumbles – a very fragile system to hold.

I don't blame my parents for my experiences, I never blamed them. They tried their best to create a safe, warm and loving home for me. They tried their best, with skills sets they had available to them to create all necessary conditions for my healthy development. They mostly succeeded. But they too were victims of family schemas they were unaware of. And because they were unaware the cycle had to repeat.

"A person is a fluid process, not a constant and static being; a flowing river of change, not a block of solid material; a constantly changing constellation of possibilities, not a fixed number of features." (Carl Rogers)

CHAPTER TWO

TEENAGE YEARS, DEATH, CRAZY, IMMERSIVE FEELING – WELCOME TOXIC LOVE AND CO-DEPENDENCY

I.
At the age of thirteen, I decided that I no longer wanted to go to private school, and persuaded my parents to transfer me to public school. Most of my friends studied there, the school was closer to home, and I wanted to experience a different environment and more independency. I did not want to be under the constant surveillance that was possible in a private school. My narcissistic grandfather was not thrilled as you can image – *"what are people going to say?", "how will it look like in the eyes of others?", "this is a terrible mistake!", "why you are so careless?" "You are so ungrateful! Throwing away such a privilege – unbelievable!"* Why would I care what other people would think about this? That wasn't my problem. I no longer wanted to play a role in the farce, in the false illusion of "our family is great, aristocratic, better, above everyone and everything." I wanted to break free from it – I wanted to be myself and make my own choices.

I will not say that it was easy to change schools because it was not. It was actually quite rough. It turned out very quickly that I had quite big gaps in some of the subjects. Suddenly I found myself in a class with almost thirty students. The teachers did not have time for an individual relationship with any student really – that was not what I expected. In a private school, my class consisted of no more than ten classmates, each teacher had time to get to know his students, and learning was more suited to the individual needs of the child. It was hard for me in my new surroundings. I felt alienated (despite having many friends in my class), worse, as if detached from reality. For some time I couldn't find myself. Kids can be really cruel at this stage I learned too. I was not bullied, but I remember one girl telling me that I have the thickest, biggest, fattest legs of all the girls in the school picture (combined with the joking term "pear", which I mentioned earlier, something shifted within me and my body image began to disturb from that moment onwards). Another girl tried to beat me up because of a rumor that I had a secret relationship with her boyfriend (I didn't by the way). Fortunately, "the boyfriend" was a good friend of mine and the matter was solved without any physical harm (I can't fight myself, so I would probably get a good spanking). Earlier, learning was easy for me – at public school I had difficulty with every homework, every new theory. Such a nightmare it was! Somehow I managed to pass the year, but I was definitely no longer the best student in school, which caused quite a lot of frustration, anger and disappointment toward myself and the idea of who I was.

II.

The following year was easier when it came to going back to school. It was tragic, however, from a personal point of view. When I was fourteen, my grandmother died unexpectedly – she had a stroke. My parents kept it a secret from me, so I would not visit her in the hospital where she was lying in the intensive care unit connected to machines that would keep her alive. I never had a chance to say goodbye to her. I know my parents didn't want me to remember her that way. It was the first and, at the moment, the last funeral I have attended. The funeral was absolutely devastating. I mean, it was also beautiful for some as the chapel was absolutely packed with hundreds of people – my grandmother was loved by many. But all I remember is an open coffin, and in it she was lying – my beloved, adored, intelligent, cheerful, funny, sociable, gypsy music-loving grandmother. My second mother. My personal hero and role model. I couldn't watch it. I fell into a state of panic, despair and hysteria. I screamed, cried, my rationalism disappeared somewhere, I had a complete emotional breakdown. My parents had to take me out of the chapel in which she lay until the coffin was closed. I just couldn't look at it, couldn't bear the pain and anger I felt. Upon seeing her corpse, millions of thoughts crowded into my teenage mind: *"Who is it? It can't be her! She doesn't even look like her – she's a stranger, not my grandmother!"* Utter hopelessness and a nightmare. I remember the feeling of horror when I realized that she would never hug me again, that she would never greet me with that mischievous smile of hers, that she would never dance to the guitar sounds she loved so much. That I would never hear her laugh again, feel her warmth and love. That she would never wave at me from her balcony again when I come home from school (she always waited for me and waved me hello, every day without exception; her block was literally in front of my school so it was the first building I saw when leaving the building). I remember the excruciating pain in my heart. I remember… black, wild, omnipresent despair, rage and void. My world collapsed at that moment. Something had broken inside me. I felt like a big part within me died with her. Fate scoffed at taking her so young – she was only fifty-six years old. She was a brave woman. She raised three boys alone. She was also unforgiving, resentful and I guess you could say a jealous woman. Grandpa left her for someone else, someone whom she offered help and support, took this woman under her own roof – can you imagine? It sounds a bit like a Spanish soap opera, but it was like that. My family was full of drama and action spins. My grandmother must not have been relieved of bitterness, loss and resentment toward him all her life. When I think about it now, I guess that's what killed her at the end – all the brewing feelings she had about his betrayal, his rejection which were never fully expressed. I found the moment she died was very interesting – my grandmother died exactly one week after my grandfather lost all his fortune. From rich to poor in one short moment – bad investment and boom! Everything was over for him. He lost his position, power, home, social status, and to some extent his family and my grandmother found peace in his loss and suffering. She left with a feeling that karma always comes back.

    I have gone through all the states of grief: denial, anger, bargaining, depression, and acceptance (based on: Kübler-Ross model). Stages can mix, occur in different order, and some may not occur at all. This is a fairly simplified description of the process, but it is the most common one. In my case the depression stage lasted the longest. Again, I have a huge memory hole about the first months after her death – how amazing what our mind can do to protect us. How quickly our mind opens up the vaults where the most painful experiences are locked up for many years. Fascinating, don't you think?

    I lost my interest in school and my grades kept getting worse. I started playing truant, I met new people. I started drinking a lot and smoking cigarettes. There was a boy in the crowd where I was hanging around. I guess we can call him my first boyfriend.

He himself was a bit lost, immature, he was quite angry with the world, a generally troubled young individual. This interesting bond between us lasted about a year. On reflection, I think we were connected by the anger and sadness we both felt at the time, we did have a lot of laughs and funny moments though. These moments helped ease the pain of loss sometimes. We rarely spent time alone – always in a group. He was several years older than me, so at some point in this relationship, he wanted something more, and I didn't want it and I wasn't ready to give it to him (after all, I was only fifteen). So he left me for another girl – this happened quite unexpectedly. I remember that I came to his house to watch a movie together and he said that he was leaving me for someone else (his next relationship didn't last long from what I can remember). Just like that, no indications whatsoever. It was the first (and the last) time anyone had left me, someone had rejected me in such a way. Another loss to add to my private collection. In retrospect, I know that this was the first conscious moment in which I felt inadequate, not good enough. Did I suffer? Sure, I did but I numbed it with different substances. And so life has become a waiting for the moment when alcohol will hit my head and I will feel relief from suffering so palpable in everyday life. I wasn't addicted to alcohol, but I was heavily abusing it. Dad had been living in England for some time at that point and hadn't seen me struggling with the loss. My mom witnessed it more or less and didn't know how to help me. I think she saw how slowly, successively, my true self fades away, and a wall is formed behind which I can hide and feel, at least a little, as if I have control over what has happened in life. She wouldn't let me leave the house when I was coming home drunk (it happened several times). I did not rebel (after all, still meek, still fulfilling expectations to some extent to be "good, perfect"), I served the punishment and then the merry-go-round started again.

These emotional turbulences lasted for about a year. After that my mother decided it was going to be enough and took me to a child psychologist. And guess what? It did help, on reflection, to some degree. I must admit that I do not remember what I talked to this psychologist about, what we were working on in detail. I can only vaguely remember that we were talking about my parents' divorce, grandmother's death, change of school and how to cope. I went to these meetings once a week for about six months. All I remember for sure is that my grades started to improve and my destructive behavior started to decline. So I think these sessions gave me something. I never told her about the sexual abuse. It was still my dirty, poisonous, disgusting secret. I didn't trust her enough to share that. It is a pity that I remember so little from these sessions – now I am very curious about how they looked like, what was said and what was left unsaid, what was about her that I didn't trust to share all my struggles. I remember one session very clearly though where I was talking about the guilt I felt about experiencing "happy moments". I felt very strongly that I should not be happy at any point; I should not laugh or have any positive emotions because I had lost someone so important. It felt like a betrayal, something unacceptable, inappropriate, shameful at times even. As if these good moments diminished the value and importance of my grandmother. I was afraid that I would forget about her if I was happy. I didn't understand it back then, and now I know that many people going through bereavement feel similar emotional torment. Feelings of guilt related to a thought of engaging with life again. Feeling guilty about the joy you might feel. Have you ever experienced pure panic in these moments when you realized that you are not thinking about the lost person in every minute of your day? I had, many times. I remember that a psychologist helped me normalize my feelings and showed that the most important thing is to remember the person I have lost. That no matter where life takes me, this important person will always be with me in my heart and memories. And she will live as long as I remember her and my love to her will be cherished – this was a stage of my grief where I started to look for a meaning in my great loss. I started to see the meaning of my grandmother's life onto mine and that helped me heal. David Kessler proposed meaning as a sixth stage of grief and I agree with him on that. It is extremely difficult to find, and/or feel meaning at the early stages of our loss. At the same time, finding your meaning to your loss can offer you a closure we all look for in our pain and suffering. My grandmother was all about helping others, being kind and loving life. And I've decided that I will honor her by living by these values every day in my life. There I found my meaning. Yes, that was an important and helpful lesson. I sincerely hope that I will continue to put effort in every day to honor, cherish, nurture my love and meaning of my grandmother's life in my everyday life. My relationship with her didn't end and it never will. It just changed a little in its form.

III.
Now... let's move to the age of sixteen to seventeen, the time of high school. The exams at the end of my previous school went pretty well and so I'd managed to get accepted into a good high school (in Poland the educational system used to look like this: nursery, kindergarten, primary school, gymnasium, high school or technical/professional school and university). I met new people – my best friend (his name is Adrian), whom I had known

since kindergarten, also got accepted to the same school, but we were in different classes. He was in the humanistic class (not because he loved the Polish language or literature, but because he felt like a doughnut in butter being amongst so many girls), and I went for mathematics and computer science. What an ironic thing. I smile as I write these words, because when I think of the choice of specialization I took (math's – IT) it could not be further away from my plans for the future (at least I thought so then). Yes, at this age I already knew what I wanted to do professionally – I wanted to become a psychologist and psychotherapist. I wanted to work with addicts – my mother was the main inspiration here as well as my grandmother (and, in a way, the experiences with my dysfunctional families). Observing my mum's personal growth and the lack of one in my dysfunctional family created fascination and curiosity within me. This field fascinated me. I wanted to know all about addiction, the nature of creating it and breaking free from it. I wanted to understand why people behave in the way they behave, what contributes to their choices, why their brains are working in specific ways. I wanted to understand humans as best as I possibly could. I had a brief period when I wanted to become an attorney, but unfortunately corruption in Poland (at least in those days) made it impossible to enter the circles of law without proper connections, so psychology won. Deep down I feel like it was always winning. Nevertheless, chosen subjects in high school helped me get into university three years later as math's was taken into account for the sake of statistics and psychological research and methodology. Such small digressions but, let's return to the main plot. High school allowed me to meet three best friends with whom I shared my further ups and downs (they are still part of my life for which I am extremely grateful and happy). Let's call them Kitty, Phil and Chris. Each of them is very unique and different from one another. Each of them helped me in different ways along my way. We had challenging moments where our friendships were almost destroyed but we always found a way back to one another. They are making my life richer in so many ways. Chris and I started to develop something romantic at the beginning of our friendship, but a year later we broke up and remained good friends until this day. Now Chris and Kitty are happily married and have a wonderful son. Anyway, Chris introduced me to the group of his friends, some of whom, interestingly, were from my previous crew (you remember people with whom I drank too much? That's the one). And this is how I met a man who changed my life forever. Let's say his name was Philip.

Philip was four years older than me, and in my humble opinion was a handsome guy (my friends would strongly disagree with me here). He had just returned from basic military service, which was not compulsory in Poland back then, but he always wanted to work in a uniform and be somehow involved in the military. This is how he saw himself, and I respected him for it. He presented himself as if he knew what he wanted in and from life and that was an attractive quality for me. He was charming, clever, cheeky. His eyes were mesmerizing. I remember the moment I met him. I just came back from London, visiting my dad. Philip approached me, tipsy already with another beer in his hand saying *"you have very beautiful eyes. I never saw eyes like that before."* Boom... I was intrigued. Some of my friends told me to be careful with him. Did I listen? At first I did. At first, we were just friends, but we got closer to each other pretty quickly. We talked a lot, went for long walks together, he shared some deep thoughts with me. He let me in into his vulnerable zone and he became something more than a friend. A few months of intimate moments like that started a growth of love... dangerous love. I was unconditionally in love with him. I was exploding from love, I was drunk by love for him. It was that moment when my personal adventure with co-dependency and toxic love began. Let me delve into this topic here and share this adventure with you more extensively.

The first year was wonderful – I think, like most relationships, we had a "pink glasses" phase, a falling in love phase, a honeymoon phase; however you want to call it. The reality was uncompromisingly great and fabulous. I idealized Philip, he was placed on a pedestal of excellence and perfection in my eyes. I did not see any flaws in him for a long time – it did not matter that he drank a lot; "*we are young, it will pass, it's just a phase*" I was telling myself over and over again. It didn't matter that we always spent our time the way he wanted – I simply did everything in the world to make him happy. Nothing bothered me. It didn't matter that time revolved mainly around his friends and drenched parties – never movies, walks, shared dinners, travels. Nothing else mattered, only he, being with him, being close to him, mattered.

According to Pia Mellody, addiction is a relationship between two people, involving the induction of intense obsessive-compulsive experiences that lead to the building of bonds so tight that they are closer to entanglement than to healthy connection. Co-dependency, on the other hand, is the result of destructive behavior emerging in the relationship on the one hand and an incorrect response to it on the other hand (this can happen in a relationship that was initially healthy). Thus, co-dependency arises as a result of the interaction between one person and the destructive behaviors of the other person. That's what happened with us – he started drinking more, showing disrespect and lack of dignity toward me, at times showed aggression not only verbal but also physical and sexual. He was becoming mocking, critical, hurtful, and I just put up with it, because it seemed to me that I loved him. I put up with all of his abuse in the name of love. I endured it because I concealed the hope that it would change, that it would be different with time. I loved him, but not with wholesome and healthy love – it was a toxic love.

Let me say here a little more about the core symptoms of co-dependency highlighted by Pia Mellody and apply it to my own experiences (symptoms listed below are based on her book "Facing love addiction: giving yourself a power to change the way you love", 1993 – highly recommended reading). There are five core symptoms of co-dependency:

Difficulty with accurate self-esteem: A person with a healthy self-esteem knows that he/she is valuable and the inner value is maintained even when he makes a mistake or when he is lied to, deceived, angry at, or rejected. Self-esteem is constant and not dependent on external factors. In a co-dependent person, self-esteem can fall into two extremes – the first is to underestimate it, and the second is arrogance and thinking about self as someone better, more unique than others (this is called megalomania). For me, it was definitely the first extreme. You have no idea how many times I had heard from Philip how helpless and useless I am, how my feelings meant nothing, and he doesn't care what I think or feel. Friends and having a good time were the most important things to him not me or our relationship – that was never prioritized. I changed everything for him – my style of clothing, hair color, I started wearing make-up so that he would only appreciate me, maybe even compliment me at least once. I adapted my whole being to him. I wanted to feel important to him. I craved to feel loved, desired, wanted and appreciated. I never got anything from him even a flower he could take from the meadow (that would mean the world to me, truly). We didn't celebrate our anniversaries, we didn't travel anywhere (sorry – I am exaggerating, we were on vacation with his parents in Croatia once and once we went to the mountains for a weekend where he proposed (he was drunk while popping the question I remember); these were the best days of our relationship pretty much). My self-esteem was going downhill and I began to consciously believe that I was ugly, not good enough, inadequate, my feelings weren't important. I didn't like to look at myself in a mirror, my self-talk became a mirror of his hurtful statements.

Difficulties in setting functional boundaries: I often explain to my clients that boundaries are like an invisible force, a protective field that surrounds us and is primarily intended to protect us from abuse by others. It also protects others from abuse by us and allows us a safe space to develop a sense of who we are. Boundaries are primarily divided into external and internal. The external boundaries are mainly physical and sexual. Internal boundaries are designed to protect our thoughts, feelings and behaviors, allowing us to take responsibility for them and separate them from the thoughts, feelings, and behaviors of others. I had no functional or healthy boundaries. My external boundaries did not exist – Philip was my first sexual partner, which of course only added him more meaning and significance in my mind, and for him I was simply someone with whom he could satisfy his sexual needs. We were not making love – well maybe the first time; it was not an expression of intimacy but rather a physical act that he benefited from. Quick, painful, emotionless act nothing else. For the most part he didn't even look at me. He raised his hand to me several times too – always knew how to hit without leaving marks. I remember one instance vividly when his father had to enter the room and hold him down because he would have strangled me to death. His father gave me the opportunity to escape. Of course I ran away, but I was still immensely in love with the guy so after a few days I came back and the relationship continued. I was judging myself for this for many years. My inner boundaries were disturbed. I didn't take responsibility for my feelings or behaviors, and if I did, I wouldn't be in this relationship for such a long time. I lost myself in it. It became a central point of my existence.

Difficulty in maintaining and expressing own reality: People struggling with co-dependency very often find that they do not know who they really are; the objective truth about themselves is distorted. There are four factors that make up our reality: body, thinking, feelings, and behaviors. If we struggle with the difficulty of expressing our reality, we may find that a person has difficulty realizing his own appearance or how his body functions; present difficulty in recognizing one's own thoughts and difficulty in communicating them to others; we are not sure about our own feelings, what we feel; there are also difficulties being aware of our own behavior – what we do and what not to do; even if this awareness is in place, there are difficulties with controlling our actions. Pia Mellody points out that the above-mentioned difficulties can be experienced on two levels, A and B, where A is less dysfunctional (the person realizes what he or she is experiencing but does not express it out of fear of the consequences). Level B is considered more dysfunctional where we do not know what our reality is; we create a "new identity" to fit into the illusory reality. I wish I could write that I was on the

A level, but to be honest I was somewhere in between these two. I was aware of my thoughts, I knew what I felt, but I had difficulty expressing them. At first I tried to stand up and defend myself, to express myself, but it always ended the same – intimidation and threat that he would leave me, physical and verbal abuse, so over time I just stopped doing it. I got lost, squashed, scared. I did not notice my own attractiveness, sexuality or femininity. When someone complimented me, I thought the person was lying because why would I look nice in something? After all, I kept hearing how hopeless, useless, ugly I am, how I should change some clothes because I didn't look like he wanted me to, make the make-up more provocative because he liked it more than delicate one – no matter that I felt like a cheap whore at times. I did it for him to make him happy because I was hoping that he would love me as much as I loved him. *"If only I change this… wear that… do this…"* Empty hopes are very typical in co-dependent dynamic – I've had a lot of them, they've held me in a trap.

Difficulty recognizing and satisfying our needs and desires: each of us has needs that must be met. Maslow very nicely and clearly presented human needs through the pyramid, which are important for each of us to ensure healthy development. When we are children, our careers are responsible for meeting our needs, in adulthood it is our personal responsibility. Some of our needs can be satisfied with the participation of other people, e.g. the need for closeness, belonging, and intimacy. Desires can be divided into small and large – small ones are our whims, while large ones give direction to our life and play an important role in our sense of fulfilment. I was aware of my needs and desires. When I am thinking about it now, I was fulfilling some of my desires: I was accepted to the university and the field of study I wanted. I remember that I had to fight for it because here Philip and I were creating a negative correlation – the more I developed, the more he turned into an aggressor/abuser. With each passing month, I had a strong feeling that the Philip I once met was disappearing forever. I perfectly remember that we were already engaged (when he proposed, I was overjoyed and my family and friends were genuinely terrified and against it. Did I listen to their advice, fears and concerns? Of course not because my illusion that it would be better, my empty hopes that he would change was more powerful than ever. We can see here very clearly, that the very same mechanism of illusion and denial is present not only in addiction but also in co-dependency. For the first time he openly shared some light on me by giving me the ring! That moment was like a sunshine just shining for me… in that moment I felt truly special) and Philip had the idea that we should start trying for a child. Can you imagine? Our relationship was in jeopardy and he wanted to start a family! No thanks… I thank the universe that I had some inner strength left within to fight for my biggest desire, for this area of my life, because if that was taken away, I would cease to exist completely. My "ME" would be totally lost. Were my needs met? Some of them yes – the most basic ones, such as a roof over my head, food, water, access to the air. The need for security was partly but mainly from parents and friends. Higher needs such as: love and belonging, self-esteem, respect and recognition, not really. Self-actualization one? Big question mark here. His problems became my problems; mine didn't matter and were neglected. He had become the center and the purpose of my little universe. I wanted to love and be loved – I did, but did I feel loved? Looking at the description above, sadly not. There was no peace in our relationship, lack of stability, only constant threats, fights and emotional blackmail. I felt like on a leash – when Philip wanted me to be close, I was. In those moments he was lovely, he spoke beautiful words, made promises full of love and change, he apologized and cried when he made a mistake, and sometimes he even begged me not to leave. He mastered manipulation skill for sure. When he did not want to, he rejected me, swore at me (you name it I heard it all), and ended the relationship only to come back a few days later and promise improvement and use his charm to bring me back. It was like a chaotic dance, and I let him lead it.

The difficulty of experiencing and expressing your reality in moderation: perhaps the easiest way to describe this difficulty is to say that the person functions at the extreme ends. Everything or nothing. Black or white. I love you or I hate you. I want to be with you or I don't want to. There is no middle ground, as description says – no moderation. Everything I described in the fourth core symptom can be also included here. This stunning, dazzling, unstable, overwhelming, intensely destructive dance. Everything was so intense, so absolute, and so explosive. I felt the highs as if the sun's rays were directed only at me. As if God chose me and only me to share a moment with. The downfalls as if someone had thrown me into a dark cellar full of shit and waste, completely closed to the world. The dark cellar was full of pain, humiliation, powerlessness, hopelessness, suffocation, despair.

For many years I did not remember this moment, but most recently, while on a spiritual journey with my Kundalini Yoga/sound teacher, I have recovered some memories from the beginning of this relationship and I can remember that Philip said to me once: *"I never thought that a person like you would even consider dating someone like me. Let alone being together with someone like me"*. Now I can see that Philip had issues with his self-worth back then (I am not sure how he is now but I wish him well). As I write all of this, I feel sorry for him and I feel sad when I think how much he wanted to be loved and how he could not express it in a healthy way. How many inner scars he carried and how his internal pain prevented him from building a meaningful, fulfilling life. His parents – great to me, were very critical to him. His brother was favored – worldly, ambitious, cheerful, warm, open, loved and cherished; family pride. Philip lived in his shadow, at least in the eyes of his parents; he was underestimated and humiliated, seen as not good enough over and over again. I will never forget how his mother told me to leave him because I did not deserve to be treated as I was. Do you think I listened? I would like to say YES, but I cannot. I can't, because I left many times, but then I came back many times. Philip was my personal drug of choice, my unique heroine. Our toxic, hypnotizing, suffocating dance lasted almost five years.

IV.

I finally broke free from that relationship in 2010. I was twenty-one at the time and I had to suffer quite a lot of physical damage to finally realize that my hopes that Philip would ever change were empty, illusory, simply false. I couldn't count on him, I was with him and at the same time I was alone. Back then, I was already working full-time and studying (also full-time). Ah... and in addition to work and studies, I was an intern at the Outpatient Addiction Therapy Center too. Mainly, I ran therapy groups for people just after detox and wanting to keep absenteeism. I loved this internship as I've learned so much. These five years were like a Swiss watch for me – the minutes were precisely measured, because every one of them was extremely valuable and precious. Life was racing at a dizzying pace. In the second year of studies, during the period of final exams for that academic year, I rushed one day from work to attend an exam. I was running down the stairs, I tripped and fell down the stairs (bloody high heels). I perfectly remember that I just got up, looked around, shook myself off and ran to catch the bus. I didn't feel any pain while rushing to catch the bus. My leg swelled to the size of an elephant during my bus journey. I couldn't really walk but somehow I crawled to the exam class. After the exam, I called my mother to come to pick me up as I was not able to stand or take a step on my own. I broke my knee and was immobilized for over six months; another six took for rehabilitation and learning to walk again. Not only was this period full of physical pain but the emotional pain too and this one was way worse.

Lying in my own bed, all I could do was read, sleep, watch movies, think and wait. I waited six months for Philip to visit me, at least once. I waited six months for a message from him in which he would at least ask me how I was doing and if I needed anything or send me any message really. This moment never happened. My friends visited me every day, took me to the remaining exams so that I would not fail the year, then they were driving me to rehabilitation – every day without fail. They watched my emotional suffering. I talked little, cried mostly. I missed Philip badly and still waited for a sign from him. Without even realizing it, I started emotional detox from unhappy, toxic love. Yes, I was addicted. The characteristics of emotional addiction were distinguished by Anthony Giddens. He lists three groups of features:

Drunkenness – an emotionally dependent person in a relationship with a partner feels that it is necessary for his/her well-being; being in a relationship is experienced as a state similar to intoxication from psychoactive substances (e.g. alcohol, drugs, medications etc.).

Dose – an addicted person needs more and more "doses" of being present and spending time with a partner. Thinking about the partner is not enough, the person needs constant and tangible evidence of attachment (e.g. reassurance that you are someone important, you are loved, wanted etc.).

Losing your own "I" – in emotional dependence is a real danger of losing one's own identity, as well as ability to make a critical assessment of yourself and the other person. The feeling of losing identity may be accompanied by shame and remorse.

Yep, that was me – clear as a sunny day. I did not have access to my "drug". It wasn't by my own choice either. I was thrown into the deep end and if it weren't for my friends and my mother, I don't know if I could have made it. I felt an emotional craving, just as an alcoholic is craving for alcohol during detox. I felt it every day, every hour, every minute, every second at first. I was angry, irritated, I felt an inner suction for a top-up. I was obsessed with thoughts and dreamed about HIM. How happy we could be; I fantasized about the future with him, explored so many different scenarios, revisited over and over again some good moments we had and so on. I was sinking deeper to my emotional rock bottom every day. I felt as if someone had ripped my heart out, my whole chest was one big void, one big wound, as if my whole self had ceased to exist. All that was left of me was this shell called the body; I was nobody. I entered into abstinence not out of my own free will. Philip made this decision for me without even realizing it. One person truly managed to get through my existential pain and that person was my oldest friend.

My best, beloved friend, Adrian, spent every free moment with me. I felt a great shame because I allowed Philip to separate me from all my friends over the years. I hadn't seen Adrian for the most part of my relationship (Philip didn't "approve" of any of my friends who he didn't know or just didn't like for whatever reason). And when Adrian found out what had happened, he just came as if we had seen each other yesterday and surrounded me with his warmth and love. I wish everyone could have such a friend. We didn't have to talk about our separation – we both knew why it happened. We also knew that nothing can change our bond. Reconnection with Adrian was like coming to a welcoming, safe and warm home. We watched movies together, ate junk food, sometimes we laughed, sometimes I cried, sometimes we talked for hours and sometimes we just sat in silence sharing the space of my little room. No judgements. No matter what we did, I always felt safe with him and accepted for who I am. It has always been like this with us – we were able to sit for hours and share our most intimate thoughts and feelings. Vulnerability wasn't scary. We had come to a stage in our friendship where we understand each other without words. We know each other inside and out as they say. He is my soul mate; we love each other with platonic love. He is like the older brother I wanted to have. We push each other toward self-improvement. Sometimes we challenge our views or beliefs but always in a supportive and respectful way – never to belittle or hurt but more to progress. I can't say that everything was going smoothly: just like craving for alcohol or drugs, emotional hunger every now and then appeared and demanded (this internal suction, sometimes is a form of a tearing pain in the chest) to plunge into regret again, get married in misfortune, stick to the thought about my most important topic, around which I centralized my whole love life. What an easy way out it was! Have you ever heard of a broken heart syndrome? A broken heart is a very common and natural stage after breaking up with someone. It is an important moment during which we are supposed to allow ourselves to experience the emotions associated with it – no matter how difficult or overwhelming they are. Difficult experiences help us to develop our emotionality. At the same time, the reduced well-being after the breakup allows us to work through the thought that the relationship has ended. Broken heart syndrome feels very similar to a heart attack. Poetry and songs about a broken heart describe this state very beautifully, but it is worth remembering that it has a physiological basis, and its source is severe stress. A broken heart manifests itself primarily by:

∞ chest pain
∞ irregular heart rhythm
∞ an increase in the cortisol level in the blood
∞ pulmonary oedema
∞ left ventricular enlargement
∞ decreased body temperature
∞ low mood, which in some cases, if prolonged, can lead to apathy or depression.

So, what helps for a broken heart? Time, first of all. The most difficult days are the first few days when our mind does not accept the situation and tries to deny the loss. Then, within a few weeks, we may experience various emotions, such as regret, anger, longing, and sometimes depressive states. The acceptance stage can appear after some months after the breakup, but it is a very individual matter (there are no specific time frames). What is worth remembering is that emotions will start to drop gradually. We can also experience mood swings and fall into euphoria from the deepest apathy, this is also a natural reaction to severe stress. All well and good, but how can we heal a broken heart? How do we deal with a broken heart when we go through our state of loneliness and pain? It will certainly be much more difficult. Some people may prefer to be alone in the first period after the breakup, but if possible, it can be helpful to try to meet family or friends as soon as possible. Perhaps it is worth considering moving in with a best friend for a few days, or maybe a sister or mother will be happy to visit for a while? Let's not be afraid to ask for support from trusted people. Initially I wanted to be on my own but it was making everything worse so I did open myself for support and company. Adrian was always supportive and gently pulled me out of this emotional sewage. Baby steps as I like to say. He was (and still is) my guardian angel. I have always liked Antoine de Saint-Exupéry's aphorism, *"Friends are like silent angels who lift us up when our wings forget how to fly."*

After about eight months of my private, emotional tragedy, I decided that it had to be over. That it's time to contact Philip and say that I am leaving, that we are done. I'm not proud that I broke up with him over a text message, but today I know that I had several (in my opinion good) reasons why I did it this way and not the other. First of all, I was still immobilized after the accident and Philip didn't contact me (I tried to call once but he didn't answer so I didn't try again). Second of all, I was afraid as hell that if I saw him, I would give in again. It's a bit like asking an alcoholic to sit in front of a bottle of vodka, hoping he won't drink it – at the beginning of abstinence it's an extremely difficult challenge, don't you think? So I wrote to him that this is the end between us and I requested that our paths do not cross in the near future. Do you think he respected my wish? When someone who was in control all the time suddenly loses it... well this can't end up well and it didn't for me. He didn't want to leave without a fight.

"We are no longer children and if we are in a toxic relationship

it is because we accept its harmfulness and we believe we deserve it. There is a limit of poison we can endure. However, no one in the world harms us, insults us, disrespects us or uses us as we do. At the same time, the limit of self-abuse is the limit we can withstand from other people." (Don Miguel Ruiz)

CHAPTER THREE

COMING OUT FROM TOXIC LOVE AND CO-DEPENDENCY, HEALING… AND RELAPSE

I.
The first year after breaking up with Philip was difficult. He was stalking me. And I was haunted by him mentally. He suddenly became the man I always wanted him to be. He started sending me flowers, remembered my birthday. He wrote beautiful messages expressing his love and that he couldn't imagine his life without me, and so on. How extremely difficult it was not to succumb to this. I did not give in. I suffered unearthly torments, but I did not succumb. I chose freedom and change. I chose me. To become a psychologist, we had to undergo personal therapy so that our unworked traumas did not affect our work with clients and supports professionals to remain objective toward the clients and their difficulties. I worked through many personal problems by myself through self-reflection and the knowledge gathered during the lectures. My mentors at the Addiction Therapy Center supported me greatly. I underwent personal therapy there which supported my personal and professional development. I learned a lot not only about the work but also about myself. Most of my knowledge about addiction, cross-addiction and co-dependency came from there; my work with people receiving treatment, and my mother was also a treasure trove of knowledge. I was on the right track – I could feel it. My internship at the center came to

an end in early 2013.

My path to recovery was not straightforward. I think it is very important to remember that change is not a linear process. It's more of a bumpy ride. At first I didn't realize that I was addicted at all (how typical, isn't it?). Complete denial. There are four stages of recovery from alcohol addiction distinguished by Stefania Brown. Let's replace alcohol with a person and here we have:

1. **Stage one – drinking/recognizing the problem:** This is the moment when the addicted person reaches for alcohol (the addicted person is still in the relationship). The most common breakthrough moment that begins the recovery process is the emergence of awareness of the problem (eureka!). Allow me to quote the words of Ewa Włodarczyk here: "*A turning point is a breaking point in a person's life, some significant event. Hitting rock bottom, surrendering acceptance of losing control over drinking alcohol, marks the starting point for change*";

2. **Stage two – transitional:** the person acknowledges the reality of addiction and admits to being addicted to alcohol (in my case, to the person). It is also said that this is the moment of acknowledging your powerlessness over alcohol and allowing the vision of a sober life. In this phase, the addicted person begins to overcome social isolation and seek help in overcoming the addiction. The addict also learns to gradually replace drinking with other healthy habits, opening himself up to information about alcoholism (or co-dependency). It is also the moment of detoxification from drug of choice;

3. **Stage Three – early recovery:** This is a continuation of the previous stage. Here it is important to strengthen yourself in the pursuit of sobriety and work on personal development. Using again the wisdom of Ewa Włodarczyk, a person addicted to

alcohol *"begins to gradually return to family, social and professional systems, changes his worldview, broadens his horizons and his awareness, starting to perceive himself and the outside world differently, and experiencing support from others"*. At this stage, it is very important to take care of mental health, including skillful and constructive discharge of emotions in stressful situations. It can be said that this stage is characterized by a very intense self-insight and commitment to activities that help fill the void after alcohol (person);

4. **Stage Four – sobriety:** This is the time when new behaviors are perpetuated. The addicted person learns to "live sober" in social situations. A person pays attention to improving emotional and spiritual development and cares about relationships with others. At this stage, you regain confidence in others and self. Ultimately, there is a complete change of lifestyle and full acceptance of sobriety as a state of body, mind and spirit. In the case of addiction to a person, here it may be possible to open ourselves for a thought about re-establishing romantic relationships with another person, but this time on different terms.

It is quite clear that I had gone through the first two stages so far. I finished my studies and became a qualified psychologist in May 2013. The first thing I did was… run away. Yes, I fled to England because I couldn't imagine a confrontation with Philip at any point. I couldn't live in constant fear of seeing him in the streets (which happened a few years later anyway, of course). My heart was still bleeding, my pain was still surreal so I took the easiest path of all – changing my surroundings and having a "fresh start" I suppose. Now I know it was the best decision of my life. I moved to London with my dad and his family, I found a job as a waitress, met a lot of great people, partied heavily, started further studies, this time at London South Bank University in the field of Addiction Psychology and Counselling. I also took up an internship at the outpatient Addiction Treatment Center and conducted individual therapies with addicts. Life had a direction, a purpose, some sort of meaning again. Slowly, in moderation, I entered the third and fourth stages of my recovery. I built new friendships, I didn't enter any romantic relationships for about two years – I wanted to find myself and reclaim what I've lost. In my free time, I went to art exhibitions, museums, partied. I kept a journal of my feelings and thoughts, undertook supervisions with my mentor which were extremely valuable and full of insights, not only on a professional level but also personal. I got to know what I like and what I don't like; my style of work was crystallizing. The relationship with Philip allowed me to realize a very important thing – what I will NOT tolerate in a relationship with another person. These experiences also allowed me to recognize and develop my personal boundaries, to some degree at least. I started slowly to accept myself, I learned what my strengths, limitations are and which traits I wanted to work on. Spirituality has become an important element of my personal development too. I gave up religion a long time ago (I was brought up as Christian); spirituality allowed me to work on trusting and letting go of aspects of life that are not controlled by me, which is in fact most of what is happening around us. As an individual, I realized that I was in control of my thoughts, emotions and behavior. I am not able to control the behaviors or thoughts of other people. I was starting to accept and like myself again, my self-confidence was slowly rebuilding. My university experiences broadened my awareness, and my worldview was beginning to change. I rejected many values that I once considered essential and created a new system of beliefs and values. I opened up culturally, I flourished professionally. I have been working very hard on perfectionism and I must admit that studying in another language really helped me with that. My original belief that I had to do everything perfectly was starting to turn into a more adequate and healthy belief – that my achievements and I were good enough. I felt a relief and a joy to appreciate myself in this way. I also noticed that my self-worth started to drift away from external factors and centered more on internal ones.

As I write all of this, I feel so grateful and pleased that so much has changed. I did not suspect that I would have to go through another fundamentally difficult experience in life. And again, it was around a toxic, abusive relationship.

II.

Somewhere in between all these upbuilding and empowering experiences, my physical health began to deteriorate. I suffered from headaches, sometimes I passed out for no reason. My hands were literally shaking like an alcoholic who is going through withdrawals. I remember feeling embarrassed a lot of the time when that happened. I felt that my vital energy was going downhill. I was always tired, I had difficulty eating. I also discovered some lumps on various parts of my body. Nobody knew what was wrong with me. I was sent from one doctor to the next; the test results were coming back normal. Only when my ex-boss saw one of the lumps on my arm, she suggested that it may be Lyme disease and this diagnosis actually turned out to be correct. I returned to Poland for two months, where I started treatment in a clinic based in Cracow, which specialized in the treatment of Lyme disease. After preliminary examinations it turned out that the disease had started to develop a few years earlier and it managed to damage my nervous and digestive systems quite severely. I had to change my diet dramatically and started long-term antibiotic therapy. No sugar, no fruits, no wheat products, no coffee, no meat or processed products, no dairy products, the dishes had to be fully cooked or steamed. My diet had shrunk to such a minimal size that at first I couldn't imagine it or adapt to it. I've been on antibiotics for a good five years. Later, I had to stop the treatment because my liver and stomach could no longer cope and look for alternative solutions.

I don't think I will ever forget the suffering I saw in my parents' eyes. Many people changed their attitude toward me and started treating me as if my diagnosis was at least terminal! As if it was the end. I hated those pity looks, as if I had suddenly become someone very fragile and weak. I hated those looks because they reflected what I felt (to use Carl Jung's vocabulary – my shadow was activated and people were mirrors of my inner state). I was angry, I felt weak and fragile, I felt a sense of loss and fear of the impact this disease would have on my life. I felt as if there was a curse upon me. My illness started to define me. I went through the same stages a third time that are experienced during grief or any loss (denial, anger, bargaining, depression and acceptance). *"Will there be any limitations in addition to diet and burdensome physical symptoms? Is it possible to cure Lyme disease? What the hell is happening? How long will I have to live like this?"*. I had so many questions and so few answers. My doctor was wonderful; she showed me a lot of understanding, patience and warmth. She always answered questions as best she could. Over the years, I got used to the rigors of treatment, physical limitations and accepted the state of affairs. But I must admit that it was not easy and it took me a long time to embrace the new reality.

The whole adventure with Lyme disease lasted for about ten years. There were ups and downs, sometimes I felt good, and sometimes I felt like crap and had relapses. These ten years had a significant impact on stabilizing my lifestyle and helped me to shape not only personal but also professional boundaries even more. Before I was ill, I worked a lot (to be honest – I would have had a few more years of this pace and workaholism in my pocket); during my illness I was not able to continue the same lifestyle. I was learning where my limits are, how much time I need to rest and relax, and how much time I can devote to work and other duties. Most of my relapses were due to not accepting my limits – now I know that. At times I didn't want to hear what my body was trying to communicate, I wanted to do more and push myself and my boundaries. The body always won. As I write about it now, my disease is in remission and I am not taking any medications any more. I support myself with dietary supplements, which have helped a lot to rebuild my physical and mental condition. My diet is more varied, my physical symptoms are mostly gone, and my vitality is at a healthy level for the most part. I maintain a healthy, balanced relationship between work and private life. I am more attentive to my own needs, not only mental, emotional but also physical.

III.

At the end of 2013, I met a man with whom I got romantically involved for the next three years. Let's call him Sal. Sal originally came from Bangladesh; we met when I was still working as a waitress, and he was a chef in the same restaurant. We knew each other by sight; we showed each other kindness and politeness.

One time he asked me on a date and I agreed. If only then I knew where it would lead me. But let's not get ahead of the facts. He was interesting to me, he was different not only for cultural reasons, but also, compared to Philip, his character was different. He seemed calm, modest, polite, romantic – a completely different man. We went on that first date and had a nice time, well mostly. The first alarm bell rang during this first meeting. He said that he had a wife and a child in his country – I, having heard this information, got up and left the restaurant instantly. For me, the meeting as well as this relationship was over. Sal ran after me claiming that he was only joking. As I didn't know him very well, I couldn't tell if he was actually joking or not, so I didn't write him off right away, I wanted to give him a chance and believe in his good intentions. Now, when I think back to this moment, it seems to me that I felt very lonely. I wanted someone to cuddle with, share my experiences and be close with. And that's how it started between us, and this time the first two years were wonderful. Sal surprised me with his romanticism, he was inventive, he tried very hard to express his feelings in many different ways. He was tender, emotional, sensitive; I felt important, wanted and valuable to him. As I was not used to such a treatment it was quite stunning for me, he treated me like a princess and his top priority at all times. Slowly, my feelings and confidence in him began to develop. I felt good with him, and in such a loving way two years passed idyllically.

After two years, Sal began slowly to change. He began to be overly jealous, possessive. He didn't want me to go out alone with my friends. After a while, when I was leaving alone, he unexpectedly appeared where I was. I didn't want to be controlled, not again. This was starting to bother me. I was beginning to feel cornered as more alarm bells started flashing.

Our sex life also began to change. Sal began to be violent and brutal. In psychological terms, rape is defined as the use of threats, physical force, or intimidation to obtain a sexual relationship with another person against their will. I was raped by him a few times. A rape victim most often goes through a three-phase response model:

The acute phase of shock and numbness: (duration from several hours to several weeks after the experience) – here we can talk about two responses to the situation. The first reaction includes fear of the perpetrator, shock, and disbelief that the event happened. The event is usually kept as a secret. Very often a person blames oneself for what happened. The second reaction reflects a detachment from the experience (dissociation); the victim is very calm, still, numb, sometimes even carefree. As if nothing happened. In this phase, feelings such as shame, helplessness, humiliation, guilt arise;

Confusion phase: when the acute phase is over, the person goes into a state of disorientation. Victim wonders how he/she can live with such an experience. Here anxiety and depression may appear, uncertainty increases, the current order of everyday life is significantly disturbed. There may be attempts to isolate from the outside world and to wipe the rape out of consciousness (so-called denial);

Reorganization phase: (the duration of this phase may take even up to several years after the experience) a gradual return to equilibrium by the person. Rape is seen as an incident that belongs to the past. A rape victim begins to make plans for the future, and may show renewed readiness for intimacy with the other person.

I went through all these phases – in the acute phase I was extremely calm. Yes there was shock, disbelief and all the feelings I described above. I very quickly cut myself off emotionally from this experience. I remember that I didn't even want to call it for what it was. This phase for me lasted several days. How can you call it a rape if the person who does it is your partner? I confided to my friend what happened, and she was the first to use the word rape. I shook off the incident pretty quickly and never slept with Sal again (well, until he'd done it again and again). I was adamant that we started to sleep in separate rooms – he agreed but didn't like it. He tried many times to enter my bed during the night. He was managing to respect my boundaries for some time and then just take what he wanted in a painful, violating, cruel way. Every time I bled afterwards. Every time I cried and promised myself that this is it. Every time I just wanted to die as death would take away the shame, pain, embarrassment, humiliation I felt. Around the same time, Sal informed me that his real name was not Sal, but Nazmul. He also lied to me about his age, date of birth and his immigration status. He was in the UK on false papers and needed help to straighten his papers to start a free life. *"This is fucking great… It can't get any worse than this"* I thought. This felt like a real knock out. I remember that, in that moment, my world collapsed for the fourth time. I freed myself from one cell just to enter another one – the second one was only more decorative. I was furious with myself, disappointed and disgusted. Furious because I didn't listen to my instincts in the first place. Disappointed and disheartened that I've done so much work on myself and it still did not save me from another painful experience, from another disappointment. I remember thinking that I SHOULD know better! By the way, the word SHOULD is very interesting. I like to work with it with my clients. What many people do not realize is that our way of thinking is subject to some cognitive "traps" or distortions if we prefer to call it that way. These mental traps can take the form of irrational thoughts that greatly influence our emotions. And the word SHOULD belongs to this group of cognitive distortions. Should is related to a disempowerment and forcefulness, expectations from others or ourselves. In my therapeutic work, I encourage people to listen to their internal dialogue or the way they express themselves to catch this word and replace it with, for example, the phrase "*I choose...*" or "*I would like to...*" (and of course "*I choose not to...*" or "*I don't want to...*") to create more empowerment as well as offering oneself a choice. Other cognitive distortions that are common include:

- ∞ **black and white thinking** (using absolutes: something is good or bad, compatible – incompatible, always – never, there is no middle ground, no "grey" area; life does not always have only two solutions to offer and situations are not always so straightforward, don't you think?);
- ∞ **so-called "mind reading"** (we think we know what other people are thinking about – very often here we create our own narrative, mostly negative, which prevents us from establishing a closer relationship with another person; here I encourage myself and the people I work with to ask questions if we really want to know what the person is thinking);
- ∞ **generalizing** (using words like always, never, every time when the situation happened only once or several times, e.g. "*I ALWAYS make a mistake*");
- ∞ **disqualifying the positives** (focusing only on the negative aspects of a given situation and ignoring the positive – for example, when the boss at work complements our speech but adds a little criticism, our attention focuses entirely on given criticism only);

- **magical thinking** (believing that certain behaviors have influenced a situation unrelated to a given act, e.g. "*bad things will not happen to me because I help others*");
- **catastrophizing** (considering each situation from a worst-case perspective).

It is worth listening to our thoughts and filtering them through an objective prism. Because our thoughts are only thoughts – they are not facts. And they are not always a true reflection of our reality.

I helped Nazmul with his papers on the condition that when he receives his visa, our paths will part ways – he agreed. He passed the application, his papers were in order and he was able to continue his life in Great Britain legally and this time without me. Our paths did not diverge easily. The worst was yet to come, and I wasn't aware of it in any way, shape or form. In June 2016, I changed my job and started working as a therapist in a Private Residential Addiction Treatment Center outside London, so I left for four days a week and lived in staff accommodation attached to the Center. This way was easier for me; I could focus on my work and separate myself from Nazmul. He didn't like it, of course. For several months I lived in a tiny room with only a crumbling bed, a wardrobe and a window, nothing else. I devoted most of my time to work, and my free time to reflection and reading. In the meantime, I was looking for a flat closer to work and eventually found a flat in a charming seaside town – Ramsgate. Unfortunately, Nazmul went with me, he did not want to leave me. Every single day he took me to the train to work and picked me up from work. I was unhappy, suffocated, trapped, fearful. Once again, I felt cornered, controlled, lost, and broken. I reminded Nazmul of our agreement and threatened to go to the police and report what happened if he didn't leave. The threat worked to some extent and we managed to set a date for him to move out – he asked for six months to be able to find himself a place to live and a job in London. I felt a hint of hope that my nightmare would end. Somehow I had to endure these six consecutive months.

IV.

In November 2016 a new member joined our team. He was quiet, introverted, sad; I could pick up a vibration along the lines of "keep your distance and everything will be all right" from him. This young, intelligent, withdrawn, lost guy turned out to be my future husband. We didn't talk much at first, but I caught him staring at me often (only later he confessed that when he saw me for the first time, he felt a deep certainty that he had met his significant other). One day he wrote me a message and we started to connect on a regular basis. Our relationship warmed up, we got closer. It turned out that he, too, was in an unhappy relationship. Our message exchange started a beautiful friendship. We were able to talk for hours, we shared our secret thoughts, and we discovered day by day who we were underneath those unhappy masks. It sounds a bit like a movie script, but it was exactly like that – two unhappy people found themselves after many life difficulties. In January 2017, we kissed for the first time and risked everything to give us a chance – losing our jobs, hurting people with whom we were involved. The beginnings were difficult. I felt a great deal of guilt and remorse because I had never cheated on anyone. The unfaithfulness was inconsistent with my moral system and values (as I found out later in life, my dad was notoriously cheating on my mother, which was another reason for their divorce; and of course, Philip did not hide his interest in other women, sometimes it happened in front of my eyes, such a charming character he was, wasn't he?). I wasn't proud of myself; I will say more, I was disgusted with myself at that moment and I made a stand by saying *"we need to stop, I can't do this"*. I told Dragos openly that I couldn't go on like this. I didn't want to break his family apart, and I didn't want to go against myself (I guess I've done it long enough in my life). I watched as each of us struggled inside, for different reasons. It wasn't long before Dragos told me that he was getting divorced and that he didn't want to go through life without me. I had mixed feelings then – on the one hand, I felt guilty again and responsible for the fact that his family system was falling apart because of me. There was also the other side of me that fell in love with this man. This love was different, felt different… calm, safe, modest, warm, without drama, stable and consistent, respectful, subtle, full of acceptance and equality. Maybe even to an outsider it could seem as boring, but for me there was a sense of solidity, steadiness, certainty, safety and security. Today I know that there are important differences between toxic and healthy love. Let me state a few of them:

HEALTHY RELATIONSHIP	TOXIC RELATIONSHIP
the behavior of partners is directed toward the good of the other person	a selfish attitude, "I" comes first on both or one side
there is freedom to nurture own passions and interests, maintain and cultivate friendships with others without fear that it will be dissatisfied by the other party, partners cultivate the principle of equality and mutual respect	there is complete dependence on your partner. Lack of freedom to make decisions and freedom of behaviors (for example: not being able to go out alone or spend time with others without a partner being present)

no attempts to change each other. There is mutual acceptance and respect for who and what partners are	constant attempts to change each other. We create a completely different image of the person with whom we form a relationship in our head, instead of loving and respecting each other as we are (distorted image of reality)
intimacy is a free choice that allows to mature and achieve the best in the relationship	intimacy is influenced by the pressure of the other person. You make love with your partner not because you want to, but because you feel you have to out of fear of abandonment/rejection
the exchange of opinions is constructive and aimed at improving the relationship dynamic	an exchange of opinions is an attempt to blame and shift responsibility onto the other person. Emotional and psychological manipulation between partners is often present in the exchange of opinions

I felt like I couldn't go through an even bigger rollercoaster of feelings – and yet here I was wrong again. The time was approaching for Nazmul to move out, the agreed six months were almost over. A few days before the agreed date, on one sunny morning I woke up at my usual time, had breakfast, and started getting ready for work – I had a morning shift that day. I didn't sleep very well the night before because Nazmul started vomiting like a cat at around two to three a.m. He vomited all over the living room and bathroom, then went back to bed and fell asleep like a baby. I cleaned the entire bathroom in the middle of the night; the living room looked and smelled like a garbage dump. I was furious throughout the night and that morning. At some point I heard the alarm on his phone going off, to which I did not react at first. After about five minutes of no reaction from him, I decided to check what was going on – *"what the hell... Why doesn't he wake up and turn off that goddamn alarm?"* I thought. I entered the room where he was sleeping and saw a motionless body with eyes popping out of its sockets staring up at the ceiling. At first, my body went into a state of paralysis, complete shock, and I remember thinking, *"God... he's dead!"* A moment passed and he began to move and make strange noises – he couldn't say a single word! I was completely terrified. I didn't know what to do. I didn't know what was happening. Something snapped inside me and I started crying hysterically and my whole body started shaking. It was a typical acute stress reaction. Now I know that, but in that moment my brain was just off. Acute stress reaction (ASD – acute stress disorder or ASR – acute stress reaction) is a natural reaction that occurs in a person immediately (instantly or after a few hours) after a traumatic event, e.g. a road accident or news about the death of a loved one. For most people, it clears up within two to three days, but the literature on the subject suggests that symptoms may persist for up to four weeks. ASD/ASR is an expression of human suffering which translates into the functioning of the entire organism. Symptoms of acute stress response include somatic reactions and a number of psychological symptoms such as:

∞ Increase in heart rate and difficulty in breathing;
∞ Nausea and diarrhea;
∞ Feeling confused, numb, there may also be great difficulty concentrating attention and performing simple activities;
∞ There may be a short-term loss of consciousness;
∞ There is a feeling of strong tension, fear;
∞ Derealization or the feeling of being cut off from reality;
∞ An overwhelming feeling of despair and hopelessness;
∞ Feeling out of control over oneself and one's behavior;

∞ Sometimes there is also anger and verbal aggression toward another person whom we are trying to help.

In most cases, ASD/ASR goes away on its own and does not require treatment. However, the emotional support of a person who has experienced an acute stress response is important, as such support is one of the most important factors in preventing the development of PTSD (post-traumatic stress disorder). If the symptoms of acute stress reaction persist for more than four weeks after the event, there is a high risk that ASD/ASR will transform into post-traumatic stress disorder – somatic symptoms disappear or weaken, and symptoms of a psychological nature persist. Most often they are "transformed": disorientation, a sense of despair and helplessness transform into symptoms such as: nightmares, day-dreaming, flashbacks, constant rumination of thoughts to a traumatic event, permanent depressed mood or irritability and outbursts of anger, emotional numbness.

After the initial shock, my automatic pilot kicked in, and without thinking, I did the only thing that was available in my mind – I called an ambulance. I also called work that I will be late (I didn't go to work that day as situation progressed). The ambulance arrived very quickly. I remember that while waiting for the medics, I alternately went into a state of numbness and bewilderment to a state of complete panic, helplessness and anger. When the medics took care of Nazmul, they informed me that he was as high as a kite. Another slap in the face – *"excuse me, what? High? But how... this is impossible..."* I couldn't believe what I heard. The medics took him to the hospital, and I searched the garbage bin without thinking – it turned out that Nazmul took four packs of sleeping pills. I never thought he would do something like that. Then I had a light bulb moment and understood why he was vomiting like a cat during the night – his body tried to defend itself and clear the poison out of his system. I felt blackmailed and totally scared. I had the feeling that I couldn't leave him now since he could take his own life – I felt responsible for what he did. Nazmul, in a way, achieved his goal – I stayed out of a sense of duty and responsibility. I stayed, but not for long. Thanks to the support I received from Dragos and my friends (which was and still is invaluable), I was able to see what was happening and that I cannot allow it. I cannot be with someone out of guilt and feel responsible for their behaviors. It was his decision and he was responsible for the consequences, not me. Not again. Besides, I couldn't look at Nazmul – literally. Each time I looked, I experienced a flashback (a recurring, uncontrolled, intrusive memory that evokes clear images, emotions, physical sensations during a traumatic event). His motionless, almost dead, face turned to me, his eyes emerging from their sockets and staring at the ceiling. I tried to explain it to him, but I don't know if he couldn't or wouldn't understand me. I again threatened that if he did not respect our agreement, I would go to the police and report everything I had been through. The threat really worked this time, and he moved out soon enough. That was the end of this relationship. For several years he tried to write to me and asked to meet me; I blocked him and never replied to his messages.

Crushed again, disappointed again, angry and sad again – that's what I felt for a good six months after the whole experience with Nazmul. I withdrew into myself, in moments of loneliness I cried over everything and nothing, I rejected the support and closeness of Dragos and other people close to me. I couldn't find or feel myself. I felt tired of the constant struggle for happiness, love, acceptance, a good life. As I write these words, I am very sad that I was not able to see what was around me and feel the love that my future husband offered (or tried to give me with all his strength). Let's face it – I have taken the role of the victim. Who is the victim? Exactly, let's explore this concept a little bit closer. The victim is a person who feels internal harm. It remains at a standstill despite the fact that it could take a step forward. She feels helpless, humiliated, hopeless, powerless, embittered, ashamed and defeated. The victim thinks in terms of "why me?", "why is everyone better, but not me?" The focus is on the problem, not the solution. The world is gloomy and black, everything in it feels like punishment and torture. Self-destruction is probably the strongest word that comes to mind. It was me on the path of destruction. I didn't get on well with Dragos, we argued very often, I pushed back his gestures of closeness. I couldn't cope with myself. I wasn't honest with myself and with him. I couldn't say that I needed time to recover and wasn't ready for a new relationship. The turbulence between us continued for another year or so.

At the beginning of 2018, I quit my job and did nothing for two to three months. Two to three months of emotional hibernation, complete shutdown. I was frozen. I was unable to work with clients. I didn't feel I could give them anything, I didn't feel like I had anything to offer to anyone really. My internal resources were running on empty. I had lost direction and purpose in life yet again. I plunged into a black hole of peculiar despair. I struggled with the fear of the future, the present seemed hopeless and pointless. The toxic, devastating cycle completed once more.

"I don't think trauma is an illusion, I have no doubt that circumstances beyond our control can shape and define us. Ultimately, we make choices, allowing ourselves to be defined by our past." (Christina Baker Kline)

CHAPTER FOUR

ANOTHER OPPORTUNITY, PROCESS OF CHANGE

I.
When I think back to this difficult period for me, the beginning of 2018, I still don't know what really happened that made me move on. It seems to me that I am not able to identify one specific event or moment *"Oh yeah! That was when everything changed"*– it was not like that. The change was subtle, quiet, gentle, successive, a little bit every day. I am one hundred per cent sure of one thing though, if it wasn't for my husband, my emotional breakdown would have lasted much longer. It was he who gave me the idea of establishing a private psychotherapeutic practice. His faith in me, the time he gave me to clean up my internal mess, tenderness and love that emanated from him every day (even though sometimes I was completely unavailable to him and even repelled his feelings) and our travels. Yes – travelling to new places. For the first time in my life I started to fulfil this dream, a dream of a little girl who wanted to travel and discover new places, cultures, customs and cuisines. Our first trip together – Rome. What a place! People were vibrant and great, heavenly food, stunning buildings and art. Being there, I felt the taste of the past, I felt gods and artists creating such beautiful works of art. My heart and soul were overjoyed to be able to experience it. And Dragos was just there with me and he was as happy as I was. It was like a refreshing balm on my soul and mind. For the first time, I had someone next to me who enjoyed being with me. For

the first time, I was with someone who refused to cage me because of their own fears, someone who trusted me and gave me the freedom to be myself and accepted me for who I truly am, someone who shared such beautiful experiences with me. Then there was Cyprus – sun, relaxation, a refuge of peace. While walking along the beach in the sunshine, I felt grateful to be there. That we are together, that I am alive. At the beginning, these moments of gratitude and aliveness were short, but each moment became a little longer, deeper. I felt my wounds begin to heal. I felt my internal resources returning – slowly but surely. Dragos also took me to Romania, and I took him to Poland, so that we would get to know and feel our roots in a way. These journeys allowed me to go beyond my thinking and broaden my perspective. My attention was no longer just focused on the problem, but time to time I was able to see the solution. I saw that the world has so much to offer and that pain can, once again, be healed. I felt that my experiences so far were only a small (significant but still small) section of my path. I was moving from a victim mode to victor. The process of change started once more. In psychological terms process of change may look like this (based on Prochaska & DiClemente):

Pre-contemplation stage – we don't see a problem here yet. We push the problem out of consciousness and stay in a state that hurts us;

Contemplation stage – here displacement and denial fades away and we begin to see the problem. The problem may be the way we think or behave, something specific that affects us in a negative, hurtful way;

Preparation stage – at this stage we make a decision that we want to change a problematic behavior or a way of thinking. We begin to figure out how we can make that change happen;

Action stage – as the name suggests here we are actively trying to change whatever we want to change. At this stage, we actively look for solutions, e.g. we seek therapy, apply various tactics/tools to modify old behavior and/or thinking. Very often here we experience the fear of change, which is a completely normal reaction to something new, to something unknown (after all, we are not completely sure how a specific change will affect our further life);

Maintenance stage – old behavior and/or thinking is replaced with a new one. At this stage, we strengthen and nurture the changes we have achieved;

Relapse – not all the models include this stage, but I do, because I believe that it is a very important part of this process. Here we are talking about a temporary return to "old" habits, a slip if you like – recognizing a return to previous habits can be a rich material of knowledge about us and what influenced it. Relapse can occur at any stage of the process. A momentary return does not mean that everything we have achieved has been lost. Remembering this was helpful for me in many difficult moments along the way.

There are no specific time frames for how long each phase can last; each process of change is specific to a given person. Sometimes the transitions between phases are not smooth, sometimes we can feel that we are stuck, sometimes we are afraid to go further – it is completely natural. After all, going beyond what we know (I call it the comfort or safety zone) requires courage and risk to explore unknown, new territory, a new way of living, being.

In April 2018, I took a risk and opened my private psychotherapeutic practice. The beginnings were full of apprehension. I was afraid that I would not succeed, that I would not achieve stabilization, that the competition was too high, and that my Polish nationality would work to my disadvantage. I lacked confidence in myself and my abilities. I started working on it.

Every day, at the end of the day, I wrote three things I was grateful for on the specific day. After a while, I added three of my traits (attributes or behaviors) that I thought were valuable or meaningful that day. It was tedious and difficult at first as my mind was focused on negative and critical thinking. Most minds do this because critical thinking can predict, assess risks and dangers. And the predominant feature of every mind is to protect us from danger, to keep us alive. I was forcing my mind to think more broadly, more objectively. I wanted my mind to be able to see not only what is critical and negative, but also what is good, unique and meaningful.

I also started to verify my thoughts – I took them "to court" (this tool comes from the mainstream of Cognitive Behavioral Therapy). Probably most of us, human beings, assume that whatever appears in our heads means that it is true and it is a good representation of our reality. We very often think that every thought we have is an absolutely true one. What a false assumption. Our thoughts, especially unpleasant, challenging ones, are shaded with our emotions – sometimes with fear, sometimes with anger, sometimes with sadness or any other challenging emotion. That is why it has become so important for me to verify the way I think. Questioning whether my thoughts reflect objective reality. I took a piece of paper and wrote the thought I wanted to question at the top of the page. Then I divided the paper into two halves and wrote down on one side all the evidence for the truthfulness of my thought (defense). On the other side, I wrote down all the evidence, based on facts that questioned the truthfulness of the thought (prosecution). After I had finished both sides, I would act as a judge and formulate my verdict. Sometimes the verdict was to simply modify the thought. Sometimes the whole thought was inaccurate. After some practice, we can see very quickly that most of the evidence on the defense side is based on emotions we feel. By contrast, the prosecutor's side focuses on factual experiences and rationality. It is a very interesting method that I used sometimes several times a day. At times it was difficult for me to see factual evidence where emotional evidence poured out of me without any problems. After all, I did not give up and kept trying. Over time, this practice became more fluid and easier to use. Below, you can see how to use this tool in practice:

Thought: *"Nothing ever changes."*

Defence:	Prosecution:
- I am always feeling sad - I am making mistakes - I suck at maintaining relationships - I am stuck in life - I am not appreciated at work	- I went to the cinema last night and enjoyed it - I was recently promoted at work and got a raise - I gained a new qualification last week - I do have a few good friends

Verdict: *"There are some things which are changing. Sometimes change feels minimal."*

I also started training in the theory of mindfulness, which brought a lot of changes in my thinking and spiritual value in my life. Jon Kabat-Zinn has defined mindfulness as *"consciously focusing attention on the present moment, without judgment"*. At first it was just another method for more conscious thinking, with time it became my lifestyle. I began to observe my thoughts even more, but this time I did not get attached to them, but rather let them pass – like clouds in the sky. My thoughts became clouds and my mind a sky where they could float. I am aware that it all sounds so simple but it was not. I remember that when I started practicing mindfulness, my mind was only able to focus for about three minutes at a time and then it drifted away to the past or the future *"what I will eat for lunch?", "remember to buy a washing up liquid", "oh gosh I forgot to send my invoice", "why did I say that?"* etc. etc. The first lesson in mindfulness is to be aware of this activity and bring your attention back to the present moment without any judgement over and over again. How frustrating it was! If I can afford one little piece of advice here, it would be this: DON'T GIVE UP. Systematic work, diligence, patience contributed to the fact that my three minutes increased to five, then to ten, and so on, up to ninety minutes, for example (recently I was able to participate in meditation for two hours – that was such a great success!). Sure, I still have moments when my mind is drifting. When I notice this happening, I come back to a basic grounding technique which focuses on using five senses – *"what five things I can see in my surroundings... close your eyes and notice four noises I can hear... three things I can touch, how does it feel to hold this item in my hand (describe it but try not to judge)? Two smells I can distinguish... and one thing I can taste (here I am sometimes offering myself a little treat and use a piece of chocolate to help myself activate this sense or take a zip of coffee)"*. I still have thoughts like *"what if... ?"* (what if game – my favorite! Thoughts like this help to develop a sense of fear and contribute to increase of anxiety levels) or *"do you remember how, when... ?"*, *"If you had acted differently then maybe..."* (analyzing the past is of course helpful in breaking free from it, expanding your awareness and understanding of why you acted how you did, but judging yourself for the actions you took back then produces shame and guilt; it also contributes to depression and lowering self-worth as your knowledge and awareness today was different from your past one – in other words, you didn't know back then what you know today). It is extremely difficult to be mindful 24/7 (I think even the Dalai Lama would agree with me here). Our mind simply doesn't work that way. But it is possible to train ourselves so that the mind works to our advantage, that we control our thoughts rather than feel that our thoughts are the rulers of our lives. Mindful living helped me to move away from living in my head all the time and be more experiential from the heart and body. Please don't get me wrong – I am not trying to promote toxic positivity and suggest that we are "supposed to feel good" at all times and suppress more vulnerable emotions (such as: sadness, anger, disappointment, grief etc.). Not at all. What I am trying to suggest is that we can learn how to be more objective in our way of thinking and perceiving. Every single emotion we are experiencing has a function, is important and meaningful. Let's not be afraid to feel whatever we need to feel. Let's learn to experience the full range of our emotions in a mindful way.

Here, if I may, I include several books where you will find many interesting exercises and teachings on mindfulness: all books by Jon Kabat-Zinn are recommendable in my opinion, Mark Williams & Danny Penman "Mindfulness. A Practical

Guide to Finding Peace in a Frantic World" (a great book that offers a practical eight week mindfulness program), Eckman Tolle "The power of now" (probably one of the most iconic reading materials out there).

Another important part of my change process was the introduction to bodywork. When we go through any life difficulties (or successes for that matter), not only our mind feels it, our body also participates in these experiences. I am a supporter of the belief that our body is a temple of information. Our body remembers everything – every touch, every emotion, every fall, burn, cut, punch; our body stores all our experiences (books worth reading on this subject: "Body keeps the score" by Bessel van der Kolk, "The body remembers" by Babette Rothschild, all books by Peter Levine). Many of us forget about it somehow. Surely I forgot that my body also needs my attention, care and support. I forgot that my past traumas had not been worked through on the somatic (body) level. I forgot that my body is part of who I am. I guess now it's pretty clear to me that I just disconnected from this part of me. I split from my body. I didn't like the way how I look. Despite my small size, when I looked in the mirror I saw a whale – huge, fat, disproportionate, just an ugly body. Let me share here with you some information about this phenomenon. Distorted body image is a negative or ambivalent attitude toward one's own body as well as negative thoughts and emotions toward it. Distorted body image is characterized by incorrect perception of it basically. The easiest way to explain it is that the person looks at his/her reflection in the mirror and perceives it differently from what it really looks like. Distorted body image is usually associated with overestimating the appearance of the body, i.e. perceiving it as larger than it actually is (so in my case seeing myself as the size of a whale even though I wear XS or sometimes smaller size clothes). We can notice this ailment, among others, in people suffering from anorexia nervosa (not in my case). It may also be the case that distorted body image is associated with its underestimation, i.e. a person perceives their body as thinner than it really is, but in the case of eating disorders this distortion occurs much less frequently. The exact causes of this disorder are unknown. It seems that the disorder is heterogeneous (diverse, in other words – it can affect any area of life). The causes of distorted body image include genetic, biological, cultural, environmental and psychological factors. According to the literature, people with a family history of Body Dysmorphic Disorder (BDD) may be more likely to develop the disorder. There are different takes on what contributes to distorted body image development. One of it is that the sources of these disorders may be related to the structure of the brain, e.g. damage to the storage of the visual representation of the body or abnormal cooperation between the two hemispheres, which reduces the possibility of "updating" the accurate body image. Generally, such disorders are complicated, and it is not entirely clear what may be causing them. One of the theories indicates that it may be related to the Gestalt – a person has a specific image of their body in their visual memory, and when this image changes, they are unable to adjust it. For example, if we have an image of our own body from the adolescence period encoded in our memory, when we were overweight for example, then we import this visual image of the body to our present body image and we cannot look at ourselves from current perspective. Another explanation for body size distortions may be incorrect body size perception related to building a visual representation of one's own body image based on specific beliefs, thoughts or emotions. Thus, distortions of the body size may indicate distortions in our cognitive processes. The environment in which we grow up and the behaviors of relatives and friends can be also important. If, as a child, we observe that people close to us devote a lot of their time to their appearance and the feedback from the environment is very important to them in this respect, we can also adopt such behavioral patterns (definitely that was how my family functioned). It seems important how the environment perceives us, e.g. in adolescence, when the body changes. We can read in the literature of this subject that people with Body Dysmorphic Disorder (BDD) (or distorted body image) often say that they have heard comments such as: *"you could watch what you're eating, you should eat less,"* or *"you're fat"*. Another reason may also be the current canon of beauty, where until recently, for example, even slightly overweight could be perceived as something bad or undesirable. And finally, a possible traumatic event, such as rape, sexual abuse in childhood, and psychological factors such as low self-esteem and low self-worth can contribute to distorted body image development.

    I thought for a long time what I would like to get involved into and what will be helpful for me to do in regards to somatic (body) work. Not only I wanted to connect with my body, I wanted to rebuild my relationship with it so I can accept it and perceive it as my friend rather than an enemy. Carl Jung, again, was very helpful to me here and I came across Kundalini yoga. Carl Jung was fascinated with the unconscious and in doing what we can to make the unconscious become part of the consciousness. Yoga was for Jung a natural process of introspection, leading to extraordinary inner experiences. He believed that what his psychology and yoga had in common was his pursuit of human transformation consisting in bringing the sphere of what is personal, i.e. individual consciousness, closer to the sphere of the impersonal, which he called the collective unconscious. The phases of the development of consciousness, described by the Kundalini yoga in the symbolism of the chakras, were interpreted by Jung as a transition from purely personal, subjective psychology to objective, impersonal psychology. We can also call this impersonal psychology super-consciousness because it is superior to individual consciousness. The symbolism of the chakras allows a description of the evolution of consciousness, since the chakras *"are a symbolic theory of the psyche that allows it to be described from the point of view of the supreme consciousness, the divine consciousness."* According to Kundalini yoga, the chakras are the seat of deities symbolizing higher levels of consciousness, and the human body as a whole is a microcosm that reflects the macrocosm. Thanks to this, it is the basic tool with which we can achieve states of consciousness beyond its egoistic, subjective form. The Kundalini energy, originally sleeping in the muladhara, rises to a higher and higher level through yoga, and in the higher chakras it awakens what Jung called objective consciousness. As long as it sleeps, however, our consciousness is completely immersed in a narrow world of particular interests that is poignantly subjective and painful (duhkha). My relationship with my body began to change slowly. My sense of strength, stability and support was growing in me. My belief that I am weak and fragile has been gradually modified to a belief that my body can do a lot and I can trust it, rely on it. It will support me when I need it to. I was building my body awareness all over again. After about a year of attending group classes, I made the decision that I would also participate in individual sessions as I still did not feel well in my body. I still had difficulty in initiating sex and to some degree enjoying it – I couldn't really feel or connect to my femininity or attractiveness. My wonderful teacher (with whom I still work by the way) introduced me to gong and sound therapy. I didn't even think my body would react so strongly to sound. Sound therapy is mainly based on the assumption that the vibrations emitted from the instruments stimulate the self-healing process of our body. They will allow us to unblock "clogged" energy channels where, for example, some damage has occurred in the body, and restore a healthy energy flow that supports the achievement of homeostasis. My individual sessions for the first time allowed me to mourn this little girl who had been hurt, abused. They unblocked the memories that I suppressed, which then allowed me to create a complete vision of what I experienced and helped to work through the trauma not only on the cognitive but emotional and somatic level. My body was crying out for my attention, and I had been ignoring these signals for many years. Emotionally, I began to feel more understanding and compassionate toward myself. I remember very well that during one of my sessions I stood up for myself and refused to believe that I deserved unfair and abusive treatment. I refused to continue being a victim. I am extremely grateful for these experiences because they have enriched me not only on a personal level but also on a professional level. On the side I was also working with various Somatic Experiencing practices on my own.

During all these years of professional work, I have met many supervisors. Some have had an edifying and developing influence on me, others not necessarily. With those who were influential and meaningful to me, our relationships allowed me to develop my self-esteem in a professional sense. Our work together helped me to recognize where my boundaries lie when working with others, where my responsibility ends and when someone else's begins, and how I want to work so that it complements my beliefs about therapeutic relationship and practice in general. Of course, not only my supervisors contributed to this. Outstanding psychiatrists, psychotherapists, and the authors of the books I read, had a huge impact on me in this field. Yalom, Jung, Rogers, Levine are just a few names that have changed me as a psychotherapist. They too have been my teachers and guides on the path of who I want to be. But the biggest teachers of them all are my clients. Each client teaches me different things every day. Don't get me wrong – this part of the journey is not complete. It seems to me that it will never be because we are subject to some process of change every day (if we are careful to notice it). Every day I try to adjust the experience to the needs of the person who is sitting in front of me, because I'm not the only one creating the therapeutic process, right? Sometimes it is easier, sometimes more difficult. I love what I do, it is my passion and time to time I have moments of disbelief that I am living my dream. Because how can I be so lucky? I do what I wanted to do and I think I'm doing it not too badly. It took me six months to be where I wanted to be. Namely, I had a full set of clients with whom I worked regularly, which allowed me to feel stable. Work has always been a great passion for me, it gave me (and still gives) a lot of joy. Thanks to working with my clients, I honed my therapeutic artistry and developed my own style of work. I have always believed that each of us is unique and exceptional. Just like our problems or the way we see, perceive, and process others and the world in general. Therefore, my style was based on matching the individual needs of my clients. Over the years, I come to the conclusion more and more often that most of our psychological difficulties are closely related with difficulties in self-worth, which is why it is a constant element of my therapeutic work. Each day gave me a chance to travel with my clients on their journeys and I feel a great honor and privilege to be part of their developmental processes. Every trip was (is) worth it. Each journey was unique and unrepeatable. I have met (and still do) so many unique and fantastic people for which I am deeply grateful every day. Maybe someday I will write a book on some of their therapeutic processes – who knows? When I started to spread my wings in the field of psychotherapy, my very first dream came back to me. One of my biggest dreams was to open a therapeutic clinic that would not only focus on the human psyche but also on the body and spirit. This dream is still just a dream but now I have a sense of the reality of this dream. I am able to see smaller goals that will allow me to achieve the biggest one. So far, I have decided to start retreats with my colleagues in the near future. Hopefully together we will be able to create unforgettable and transformative experiences for many people who suffer.

Today, while I write these words, I can say with a clear conscience – I was so wrong. I was so wrong about so many things. I believed in the stories I told myself that weren't necessarily true. Everything I wrote above is still going on, that is, I am still working on myself, I am still learning about myself and I am still solving the complicated stories of my life. I can't say *"okay I've been doing it all for a month and boom! Transformation complete."* Each day is a new beginning for me, every day I have the right to choose how I want to live, how I treat myself and what choices I make. Now I choose differently.

II.
Let's stay a bit longer in 2018, because the interesting events are not exhausted yet. My mother had her fiftieth birthday that year

and she organized a family re-union party, so I did not have any excuse to avoid meeting my "alcoholic grandfather". And I must admit I was very shocked when I saw him. He was all grey, he looked well... not how I remembered him (as I write about it now, I'm sure that my inner child was expecting some resemblance from the past). Entering my grandparents' apartment, I could feel my body filled up with fear, my body was ready to run away as quick as possible. My body was in a flight mode. When our eyes met for a microsecond, suddenly reality stopped. Then everything came back to life and for the first time in my lifetime I saw a kind of warm feeling in him, maybe he was moved to see me? I do not know exactly. Surely I saw tears rolling in his eyes. I'm not sure what was going on for him, but I felt sorry to see the old man. He has lost his vigor, strength and power. There was only an elderly man left, with some of the characteristics of that man whom I remembered from the past. I was surprised not only by his reaction, but also mine because I felt compassion. My feelings of hurt, anger, even hate at some stages in life, just went away, and only compassion took their place. He didn't seem so scary any more. My fear disappeared, my body relaxed and I no longer felt threatened. I remember thinking *"what has happened to him?"* Afterwards, I often wondered what story he was carrying on his shoulders. What did he experience, what influenced who he was, what his drinking soothes and hides? I never knew the answers to these questions. He never told his story to anyone really. I mentioned my inner child a few lines before – I am a great supporter of working with the inner child. Inner child, it is such a part of our "I" which (in my opinion) remains interested in the world forever, is open to new experiences, bold, pure, innocent, sincere, free, willing to gain new knowledge about the surrounding realities, fully focused on the present moment, each experience is unique, wonderful and special – just like little children when they are born. In other words, the inner child is you when you are enjoying a visit to an amusement park or aqua park, going out for ice cream or searching for a new book in a bookstore. It is the joy of roller skating, taking a good photo or receiving a gift. It is also unpleasant, but also very childish emotions related to the fear of being criticized by the boss, the shame of saying something not entirely "correct" in the workplace or the fear of rejection in a relationship. The inner child is that part of us that we hide in fear of being hurt. However, by hiding it, we also give up positive emotions – happiness, joy and creativity. In the case of unworked trauma during childhood or adolescence, this part of us stores the emotions that accompanied us during the traumatic event (no matter if the traumatic event took place twenty years ago – this part will feel it as if it happened yesterday with exactly the same intensity). In my case it was fear, shame, hurt, confusion, anger sometimes turning into hatred, feeling not good enough/not girly enough. Because my grandfather was an adult, I also felt overwhelmed by the intensity of his emotions; he and his behaviors were beyond comprehension in my childhood mind. Everything he did seemed to outgrow me. Each of us has an emotional past and an inner child who has reached various stages of development. Some people, thanks to their parents and guardians, can take care of their psychological wounds in adulthood and have contact with all their emotions, for others it is much more difficult. However, it is worth not to give up and help your inner child discover unmet needs. How to take care of your inner child?

    ∞ First of all, don't pretend it doesn't exist, acknowledging your inner-child is an important step of the healing

process;
- ∞ Secondly, don't be ashamed to talk to your inner child. By taking away its voice and the right to fear, sadness and shame, you also lose the positive aspects of childhood – joy and spontaneity;
- ∞ Learn to recognize the emotions of the inner child. Most often it is activated under stress; when you remember difficult situations from childhood, you might feel tired or sick for example. Perhaps you can list these situations and describe your reactions to them. Separate a child's inner emotions from that of an adult self. You can also look at your past photos. It will be easier for you to feel the emotions of your young self. Ask your inner child how he is doing. Repeat to your inner child what you wanted to hear in the past, if these messages were missing from the parents for example. Tell him that you are here for him, that you are accepting him, that you care for him, and that you will never leave him, that you will protect him now and have his back. Remember, that you can send these messages not only with words but also as emotional messages. Perhaps closing your eyes and imagining that you are hugging this little child with e.g. care and safety can be also a very powerful way to communicate with this younger part of you.
- ∞ Allow yourself to appreciate your achievements and rewards (no matter how small or big they are);
- ∞ Try not to judge and attack yourself for all your failures/mistakes (perhaps you could even reframe seeing something as a mistake/failure and instead look at these moments as an opportunity to learn/grow). Try to treat yourself gently and with understanding instead of

judging;
- ∞ In difficult moments, you can help yourself with affirmations. What would your inner child want to hear? *"You can do it", "Don't be afraid", "What can I do to help you calm down?"* – offer yourself support when you need it;
- ∞ Try to remember what you enjoyed in your childhood. Maybe riding a bike or reading books or molding clay? Try to make time for these activities and re-engage with them. These are only some suggestions for how we can re-connect and take care of our inner child.

I worked on with my inner child for quite some time and in that moment, when I saw my grandfather after so many years, I was ready to stand up for this little girl and not let her continue to be bullied and humiliated by him anymore. It was not necessary because my grandfather said nothing. He just stared at me with that unprecedented expression on his face. So, after so many years of separation, instead of a powerful aggressor, I saw who he really was – an unhappy man who could not cope with his own inner demons. At that moment, my inner child stopped being afraid and found peace. Part of my inner child healed thanks to that experience as well as protection I offered to myself in that moment.

III.

2018 turned into 2019, to some degree unnoticed, and that year was not entirely a bed of roses either. There were many difficult moments, mainly on a private level. Dragos was not happy where he worked and he wanted to change that. I remember that I was afraid because an old fear came back to me - that all financial obligations would fall on my shoulders. For several years I paid for everything myself when I was with Nazmul (as you can imagine London's life is not cheap) - I was frustrated then, I worked very hard so I was constantly tired which did not help my health. I didn't want to repeat this experience so I wasn't thrilled when Dragos was saying more and more that he will quit his job. For several months we argued quite often and could not find compromise on this. I felt guilty about how I felt, and I was aware that Dragos knew it. Time passed and he eventually quit his job, we were on shaky ground for a while. The scenario from my past repeated itself, thankfully only for a short period of time. Dragos quickly got back on his feet and found himself in a place where he feels appreciated and valuable. But I will not hide the fact that it was a trial period for us as a couple. Some of my old wounds started to hurt again, which contributed to our frequent conflicts. This conflictive time however was a great opportunity for me to work on myself; primarily I was able to work on how to be in a healthy relationship with another person. Building a healthy relationship was foreign to me, something I hadn't really experienced before. I felt a bit like I had been released from prison after a long time. The world seemed new, quite a lot has changed in it and I didn't quite know how to find myself in it again. One of the biggest areas of work for me was communication. Some of our attitudes strengthen the conflict, others eliminate it. Several attitudes that in my opinion, and based on the literature on the subject, reinforce conflictive behavior and can lead to relationship destruction are: criticism, sarcasm, defensiveness, contempt, and avoidance/withdrawal. Probably most of us have used criticism toward the other person at some point in our lives. I definitely had a tendency to do this as well as to show contempt and withdrawal. Here you go - that means most of the unhealthy conflict attitudes. I have occasionally made cruel insults at Dragos (which I was not proud of). I showed dissatisfaction when his behaviors did not meet my expectations (I could be extremely contemptuous at times). And when the situation turned out to be too difficult for me to grasp, I avoided and closed myself emotionally to his arguments. You probably know the term "silent treatment" – I have a PhD in it. He, on the other hand, repaid me with sarcasm, which was extremely painful for me. I was more used to showing contempt (showing anger, hostility toward me was quite common in a relationship with Philip as you know already). So when Dragos showed anger, I knew where I was and how to act. It was, after all, familiar territory to me. We both used far too much blaming, had a hard time taking responsibility for our actions and being open to receiving any sort of feedback. But slowly, together, we started the path of learning how to express our needs and emotions in a healthy way as well as how to communicate in a more constructive way.

I cannot say how the process looked like for him, but I can write about mine. I started my process by evaluating my boundaries – again (I wrote about them earlier). I spent some time wondering what is important to me, what my values are today because sometimes values can change throughout our lives and our personal boundaries are primarily built on them as we know. Let me share here what I started to change in my way of communicating:

- ∞ I focused on stopping using "you" and, instead of using the language in which I blame and attack the other person, I transformed it into "I" (by changing this I started taking responsibility for how I feel and what I think). Let's use a practical example here to better illustrate it:

– instead of saying *"stop treating me like a fool! You are so arrogant!"* (quite a direct attack on the other person, isn't it?);

– I started to form sentences like this: *"I feel angry when you criticized how I think about a given topic."* (not a bad difference, right?).

I remember this formula: *"I* feel (*the emotion I feel at the time*) when you (*reference to the specific behavior of the other person that contributed to our emotion*)".

∞ Another thing I tried to work on was directing my attention to the problem, not to the person it concerns. Focusing on the problem allowed me not to blame the other person and eliminate personal attacks on the person involved in a conflict situation.

∞ Reflective listening was the next aspect that I worked on. In a conflict, we often focus not only on what we mean and what we want to express, but also on making the other person take our point of view. We completely forget about listening to the other person's position. We feel misunderstood, what makes us angry and creates a sense of rejection. I am not surprised that we could not communicate if we were only interested in what was happening to us personally, and completely neglecting understanding each other.

∞ As I mentioned earlier, sometimes the arguments overwhelmed me and I couldn't deal with them – then I stopped talking and withdrew into myself. When I felt so overwhelmed with emotions, I needed time and space for my emotions to decrease to a level where I was able to control them and not turn into an abusive screamer (this is a state where "all I see is red" and no rational arguments can reach me really). And so I learned to recognize when I need a "break" from the argument. In other words, I needed to take "time out". There is a small problem here – at the beginning I managed to communicate that and that's what I need, but Dragos was not able to accept it, so it ended up me either completely shutting down and not talking to him for five consecutive days or turning into abusive screamer and not speaking for five days afterwards anyway. So the little catch here is – both sides need to learn to respect each other and respect the other person's needs.

∞ Compromise – something completely foreign to me, new, previously non-existent. If, despite all attempts, we were unable to come to an agreement on something, we began to look for a compromise solution, where both sides will be satisfied with the result. As my opinion was not taken into account before, the compromise was a kind of liberation for me from oppression. I felt bolder in expressing my opinions and despite the fact that it was not always "my way", I felt included in the decisions we made. I felt like being in a relationship where equality is just as important as respect, love, devotion, trust.

∞ The last object of my work was again self-esteem and self-worth – mostly showing affirmation, appreciating and noticing strengths and accepting compliments. I had a big problem with that… but I started with a simple step – when I heard the compliment, I would say "thank you". Don't get me wrong, my whole existence was twisting to answer some quibble "*ah you know… this is a cheap blouse from Primark*" or "*I have more make-up on than usual that's why I look different*" or any other excuse I could find in my head to brush the compliment off. But over and over again I tried to hold back and just said "thank you" instead. At first, I felt uncomfortable, strange, awkward. It became easier and more natural over time. I even started to believe some of the compliments! Shocking! How funny it is to realize that we, mental health professionals, do not have it all sort it out and "worked out", don't you think? That, we too, are only humans who have conflicts, our lives are not perfect and we also have to learn how to communicate effectively with others.

And so 2019 has passed. A year full of ups and downs, a year full of learning. Let's move now to the most recent years, to the years when something none of us fully expected happened – the world stood still for a moment due to the global pandemic. I just think that the topic of pandemic and emotions connected to it is the topic of the next book, perhaps. However, I would like to point out that it was a very busy period for mental health; many of my clients felt disorientation and fear of the unknown, which is a completely natural reaction to such a global change and invisible threat at the end of the day. For many of us, life has pushed a pause button – no travel, no socializing, no favorite coffee or whatever experiences made us smile. Suddenly, all distracting activities were gone and we were left on our own, with our thoughts, fears, anxieties. For many, it was a time of reflection, a time where some of us faced something we didn't want to face. For many, it was a time of evaluation of what is really important to us in life – for me it was such a time. I don't remember exactly when, but somewhere in 2020 my "despotic" grandfather reconnected with me via Facebook and we maintained the contact after many years of silence. His messages were full of love, and he began to show interest in my life without criticizing me for not making a fortune in banking or whatever department he wanted me to be in. I remember having a thought, a sense, a gut feeling if you like that he was dying… I don't know, maybe he knew then… but he died indeed in 2021. As far as I can tell, he had some heart condition, and then he caught Coronavirus which his heart could simply not handle. He died suddenly, unexpectedly, alone in some remote hospital in Poland. I haven't been to the funeral, no one has been as it happened during the hard lockdown. I had mixed feelings. On the one hand, I felt grateful that we had reconnected before he passed away. I felt at ease thinking that we exchanged some loving and warm words with each other. On the other hand, I had a feeling of "unfinished business", something incomplete. I missed the closure. This is a fairly common feeling experienced in grief – sometimes this feeling is so strong that action is needed. So, I decided to write a letter to him. It was a farewell letter. At first, the letter was filled with reproaches (definitely my inner child got behind the wheel there) that he had never accepted me for who I was and my life choices. That he was never happy with any of my decisions because they were not what he expected. That I was never good enough no matter how high I went or what I did. That he never accepted my partners (over the years he showed contempt and criticized in front of other family members that I brought disgrace to "our good family"). I expressed anger and hurt that he didn't protect me when I needed him to, that everything was always solved with money and not showing feelings. That he had abandoned my beloved grandmother, leaving her alone with three boys to raise. After all the regrets, disappointments, hurts were released the letter began to take on a liberating, more forgiving and compassionate character. I am not talking here about forgiveness in religious context, but more a psychological one. We often confuse forgiveness with reconciliation, and forgiveness is not the same as accepting those who have hurt or wronged us. Forgiveness (in psychological context) is defined as a conscious decision to let go of anger, hurt, resentment, and also the desire for revenge, regardless of whether or not someone deserves our forgiveness. Sometimes, we think that forgiveness is forgetting a wrong-doing, coming to terms with what has happened to us, it is an indirect saying: "in fact, nothing happened." Nothing could be more wrong. Forgiveness doesn't mean you have to forget or deny your experiences. It's not like we forgive and forget how someone has hurt us. People who have been used, neglected, abused or humiliated do not forget their traumas and forgiving doesn't mean that we need to do so. We can learn to forgive and thus remember very well the harm that has been done to us. Forgiveness is not to minimize the wrong-doing. Do not be afraid that when you forgive, it is as if you are minimizing the harm you have suffered. It does not work like that. When we forgive, we don't say, *"all right, it wasn't that bad."* Remember that you are doing this process to free yourself and not to justify your abuser. Forgiveness is also not a sign of weakness. It seems to us that by forgiving we give in, we agree with the one who hurt us. We surrender and remain the victim. Remember that forgiveness is not naivety and stupidity – it is maturity and willingness to move on. Only mature people are able to forgive and go on anyway. Sometimes I hear that forgiveness is underrated. And it's best to understand it right away. We cannot expect the person who has hurt us to understand and appreciate our willingness to forgive. What's more – we cannot expect that whoever wronged us will admit that she/he made a mistake, that she/he did something wrong. Remember that you forgive for yourself, not for others, you do not need them to do so. Forgiveness is a process (sometimes lengthy one). Forgiveness is not an event where you say to yourself *"right... I just forgive like this and that's it, done."* Forgiveness is a process sometimes we do on daily basis; we may never be able to fully forgive a person for what they have done to us (and that's okay). But we may come closer to forgiveness, let's say on a scale of one to ten, we might rate our "level of forgiveness" at seven or eight. That will be a great progress. Forgiving is something you do for yourself and that is something really important to keep in mind. When we don't forgive, we accumulate anger, resentment, hatred. The Buddha used to say that holding your anger inside you is like catching a hot, burning coal and throwing it at your tormentor. It's just that you are burning, hurting yourself while holding this coal... Research shows that unexpressed anger can be toxic to health and well-being in general, and no one wants to be with those who are constantly angry, outraged and rude... So, perhaps it is worth considering forgiving? Learning to forgive is very difficult and arduous. Because it is difficult for us to let go of anger, it is difficult to look forward without clinging to the past – and we are most often held in it by resentment and rumination on wrong-doings. Forgiveness is not easy, but those who decide to do so, who will shed anger, who will forgive, will go on and not allow themselves to become a victim again. As mentioned above, forgiveness is a process, sometimes a lengthy one, and we can distinguish four stages of it:

The Uncovering stage: during the first phase of forgiveness, we will improve our understanding of the injustice, and how it has impacted our life so here we basically can tune in into our emotions and write for example a "resentment list" (so situations, behaviors, words, gestures, everything we feel angry/resentful of);

The Decision stage: during the second phase, we will gain a deeper understanding of what forgiveness is, and make the conscious decision to choose or reject forgiveness as an option. Here we can explore how we understand forgiveness, what pros and cons we can see for forgiving/not forgiving and what could change for us/in our life if we choose to forgive;

The Work stage: during the third phase, we will start to understand the offender in a new way, which will allow us to widen our feelings toward the offender and ourselves. Here we can think about the offender's background, for example, so *"in what kind of environment this person grew up?"*, *"What contributing factors we can see for why this person behaves in this way and not the other?"* (we are trying to activate empathy toward the offender here but remember – we are not condoning!);

The Deepening stage: During the final phase of forgiveness, we will further decrease the negative emotions associated with the injustice. We may find meaning in the experiences, and recognize ways in which we have grown as a result (here, we are thinking about what kind of changes we can see within us as a result of the experience so, for example, for me the biggest meaning of my experiences is the fact that I can use them in supporting others, they shaped me to whom I am today and what line of work I am doing – my empathy and compassion levels are greater, my mental and physical health are looked after etc.).

When I finished my letter, I remember feeling internally that the "little me" and the "teenage me" felt satisfied, that they were no longer sad and angry, they stopped crying and hurting. I felt as if all my "I" merged together and my inner self was filled with peace and contentment. I burned this letter in the fireplace in my new home. I watched the words turn to ash and fly up the fireplace. I said my goodbye and healed old wounds once more. To make it easier to visualize, below I am presenting a table about what forgiveness is and isn't (highlighted stages as well as the table below are taken from the website www.therapistaid.com, based on: Enright, R. D., & Fitzgibbons, R. P. (2015). Forgiveness therapy: An empirical guide for resolving anger and restoring hope. American Psychological Association; Satne, P. (2016). Forgiveness and moral development. Philosophia, 44(4), 1029-1055).

FORGIVENESS IS	**FORGIVENESS ISN'T**
∞ Letting go of resentment, anger, hostility, fear toward someone who treated us unfairly, even though we are completely justified in having these feelings ∞ Recognizing the wrongdoer is human, and decide to treat them with decency despite what they did ∞ A chance to amend damaged relationship if we choose to do so ∞ A mental shift (or change of heart) that develops over time ∞ A process that can start at any point in time. We can forgive a person even though she/he is no longer present in our lives ∞ An opportunity to heal. Forgiveness can reduce symptoms of trauma, anger,	∞ Condoning, approving of, or excusing what happened to us ∞ Forgetting how we were wronged, or pretending like nothing happened ∞ An agreement to continue a relationship as it was. After forgiving someone, we can choose to resume, modify, or end the relationship ∞ Simply saying "I forgive you" without meaning it. In fact, we can forgive even without saying so ∞ Something we do for the other person. Forgiveness is solely for us ∞ Getting even or getting revenge. Getting even might feel good in the moment, but unlike forgiveness, it does not resolve anger and resentment we have

| anxiety, depression. It can also increase hope and self-esteem
∞ A personal decision that only we can make for ourselves. No one can make us forgive another person	∞ Something that can be forced. Just because we want to forgive doesn't mean that forgiveness has been accomplished

So here we have my story... my life changing moments... my traumas and learning possibilities. Hopefully, I have managed to demonstrate how impactful certain people, environment, experiences, decisions can be. I think that is where I will end my story. It feels like a good place. My journey is not over yet. I choose differently every day; I work on myself every day. Sometimes I am successful, sometimes not completely. I am on the path to self-discovery and self-improvement all the time. I believe that each of us has the potential and internal resources to go through such journeys. I believe that each of us can forgive past wrongs if we choose. I am not saying it is simple. But I say this: I believe it is possible. I believe that each of us deserves a different ending – one that we choose and create ourselves. I believe that each of us is special, unique, and unrepeatable and that each of us has the power to change. Sometimes we can make this change ourselves; sometimes we need someone who will believe that we can make change happen, someone who will believe in us. I believe, do you?

"I often advise myself and my clients to imagine their lives in a year or five years' time and to think about the new regrets that will arise during this time. And then I ask them the question: 'How can you start living now without creating a new one? What do you have to do to change your life?'" (Irvin Yalom)

REFERENCES:

Anonymous A., (2002). *Alcoholics Anonymous: The Story of How Many Thousands of Men and Women Have Recovered from Alcoholism – The Big Book.* Alcoholics Anonymous World Services 4th Edition

Carnes P.J., (2001). *Out of the Shadows: Understanding Sexual Addiction (3rd Edition).* Hazelden Publishing

Farringdon K., (2002). *This is Nicotine (Addiction).* Sanctuary Publishing Ltd

Mellibruda J., (2002). *Psychologiczna koncepcja mechanizmów uzależnienia.*
http://www.psychologia.edu.pl/czytelnia/50-artykuly/675-psychologiczna-koncepcja-mechanizmow-uzaleznienia.html

Mellibruda J., Sobolewska-Mellibruda Z., (2006). *Integracyjna psychoterapia uzależnień. Teoria i praktyka.* Warszawa: IPZ

Mellibruda J., (2012). *Psychologiczna problematyka uzależnień od alkoholu i narkotyków.*
http://www.psychologia.edu.pl/czytelnia/50-artykuly/1042-

psychologiczna-problematyka-uzaleznien-od-alkoholu-i-narkotykow.html

Mellody P., Wells-Miller A., Miller J.K., (2003). *Facing Love Addiction: Giving Yourself the Power to change the way You love (1st Edition)*. Harperone

Osiatyński W., (2007). *Alkoholizm I GRZECH, I CHOROBA, I...*. Warszawa: Wydawnictwo Iskry

Osiatyński W., (2009). *Alkoholizm. Grzech czy choroba?* Warszawa: Wydawnictwo Iskry

WHO, (1992). *ICD-10: The ICD-10 Classification of Mental and Behavioural Disorders: Clinical Descriptions and Diagnostic Guidelines*. WHO

Zimbardo P.G., Gerrig R.J., (2009). *Psychology and Life*. Pearson